200
Ramen Noodle Dishes

Toni Patrick

GIBBS SMITH
TO ENRICH AND INSPIRE HUMANKIND

First Edition
16 15 14 13 12   10 9 8 7 6 5 4 3 2 1

Text © 2012 by Toni Patrick

Published by
Gibbs Smith
P.O. Box 667
Layton, Utah 84041

1.800.835.4993 orders
www.gibbs-smith.com

Designed by Renee Bond
Printed and bound in China
Gibbs Smith books are printed on either recycled, 100% post-
consumer waste, FSC-certified papers or on paper produced
from a 100% certified sustainable forest/controlled wood source.

Library of Congress Cataloging-in-Publication Data:

Patrick, Toni.
  200 ramen noodle dishes / Toni Patrick. — 1st ed.
      p. cm.
  Includes index.
  ISBN 978-1-4236-2451-6
1. Cooking (Pasta) 2. Noodles. 3. Cookbooks. I. Title.
  TX809.M17P377 2012
  641.82'2—dc23
                          2011038788

Contents

Helpful
Hints

1. Extra uses for ramen flavor packets:
   - Add to water while preparing any noodle or rice for extra flavor
   - Use instead of bouillon—add 1 packet for every 2 cups of water
   - Use to flavor gravy—stir into pan drippings along with flour or whisk in water for use instead of stock
   - Shake and bake for potatoes
   - Cutlet, chop, and fish coating—mix 1 packet per 2 tablespoons of flour for coating
   - Mix with bread crumbs for frying
   - Season ground meat for burgers, meatballs, and meat loaf—mix 1 packet per pound of ground meat
   - Seasoning rubs for chicken, steaks, and pork chops

2. Check ramen packaging for vegetarian or vegan manufacturers. Just because it is labeled as vegetable ramen does not mean animal products were not used in the manufacturing process.

3. Salt lovers beware. Taste before throwing in those extra dashes—the seasoning packets are salty.

4. To reduce fat and calories, substitute reduced-fat foods such as skim milk, light or fat-free sour cream, and light or fat-free cream cheese.

5. One clove garlic equals one teaspoon minced garlic. This is much more cost effective than bottled minced garlic.

6. Two tablespoons dehydrated minced or chopped onion is equal to $1/4$ cup fresh minced onion.

7. One tablespoon dried herbs is equal to $1/4$ cup fresh herbs.

8. Fresh or frozen vegetables, steamed, can be substituted for canned vegetables.

9. As always, be creative! Most ingredients can be adjusted to your own liking.

10. To cook noodles, follow the directions on the package unless recipe says otherwise.

Soups

Summer Garden Soup

Makes 2–4 servings

1/2 cup chopped onion
1 cup julienned zucchini
1/2 cup chopped carrots
1/4 cup butter or
    margarine
1 teaspoon basil
2 packages beef ramen
    noodles, with
    seasoning packets
4 cups water
1 cup green beans
1 cup chopped tomatoes

In a large frying pan, cook onion, zucchini, and carrots in butter and basil over medium heat until vegetables are tender. In a large saucepan, combine cooked vegetables, noodles, water, green beans, tomatoes, and seasoning packets. Bring to boil and simmer 5 minutes.

Southwest Vegetable Soup

Makes 2 servings

1 (10.75-ounce) can
   tomato soup,
   condensed
1 cup water
1 (10-ounce) can
   enchilada sauce
1/2 cup corn
1/2 cup green beans
1/2 cup canned kidney
   beans, rinsed and
   drained
1/2 cup salsa
1/2 cup chopped cooked
   chicken
1 package ramen
   noodles, any flavor,
   crumbled
Tortilla chips
Monterey Jack cheese,
   grated

In a large saucepan, combine tomato soup, water, and enchilada sauce. Cook over medium heat until hot. Add vegetables, salsa, and chicken. Simmer 15 minutes. Add crumbled noodles and simmer 3–5 minutes more. Serve topped with chips and cheese.

Minestrone

1 package ramen
  noodles, any flavor
1 (10.75-ounce) can
  tomato soup,
  condensed
8 ounces spicy smoked
  sausage, thinly sliced
1/4 cup cooked sliced
  celery
1/4 cup cooked sliced
  carrots
1/4 cup peas
1/2 cup green beans
1/2 cup canned kidney
  beans, rinsed and
  drained
Salt and pepper, to taste

Cook noodles in water according
to package directions. Do not
drain. Add soup, sausage, and
vegetables. Simmer 5–10 minutes,
or until vegetables are tender.
Add more water by tablespoon if
soup is too thick. Season with salt
and pepper.

Tomato Noodle Soup

Makes 2 servings

**1 package ramen
    noodles, any flavor**
**1 (10.75-ounce) can
    tomato soup,
    condensed**

Cook noodles in water according to package directions. Do not drain. Add soup. Simmer 5 minutes, stirring occasionally.

Creamy Mushroom Soup

Makes 2 servings

**1 package ramen
    noodles, any flavor**
**1 (10.75 ounce) can
    cream of mushroom
    soup, condensed**
**1 cup sliced fresh
    mushrooms**
Salt and pepper, to taste

Cook noodles in water according to package directions and drain. Prepare soup as directed on can. Mix noodles and soup together. Add mushrooms and simmer 5 minutes. Season with salt and pepper.

Corn Chowder

Makes 2–4 servings

1 package ramen
    noodles, any flavor
1 (1.8-ounce) package
    dry vegetable soup
    mix
2 cups milk
1 cup water
1 (15-ounce) can
    creamed corn

Combine all ingredients in a large microwave-safe bowl. Cover and cook on high for 8 minutes.

Creamy Chicken Noodle Soup

Makes 2 servings

1 package chicken
    ramen noodles, with
    seasoning packet
1 (10.75-ounce) can
    cream of chicken
    soup, condensed
$1/2$ cup diced onion
$1/2$ cup sliced carrots
$1/2$ cup sliced celery

Cook noodles in water according to package directions and drain. Prepare soup as directed on can. Add seasoning packet and vegetables to soup. Cook over medium heat 5–10 minutes, or until vegetables are tender. Add noodles and simmer 2–3 minutes more.

Chicken Soup

2 sweet potatoes, cubed
1 onion, chopped
1 (16-ounce) bag baby
    carrots
6 boneless, skinless
    chicken thighs,
    cubed
$1/2$ teaspoon dried thyme
    leaves
$1/8$ teaspoon pepper
6 cups water, divided
2 packages chicken
    ramen noodles, with
    seasoning packets
2 bay leaves

In a 4- to 5-quart crock-pot, layer the sweet potatoes, onion, carrots, and chicken. Sprinkle with thyme and pepper. In a small bowl, blend 1 cup water and seasoning packets. Pour over chicken and vegetables, add bay leaves and remaining water. Cover and cook on low for 7–9 hours or until vegetables and chicken are tender. Remove and discard bay leaves. Stir in noodles and cover. Cook on high 10–12 minutes or until noodles are tender, stirring once during cooking.

Chicken Consommé and Noodles

Makes 2 servings

2 cups water
1/8 cup diced onion
1/8 cup sliced carrots
1/8 cup diced celery
1 sprig parsley
1 small bay leaf
1/8 teaspoon thyme leaves
1 package chicken ramen noodles, with seasoning packet

In a medium saucepan, heat all ingredients except noodles and seasoning packet to boiling. Add seasoning packet. Reduce heat and simmer 30 minutes. Strain liquid into a separate container. Add noodles to liquid and cook 3 minutes, or until noodles are done.

Curried Chicken Soup

Makes 8–10 *servings*

2 large carrots, diced
2 large celery stalks,
    diced
1 small onion, chopped
3/4 cup butter or
    margarine
3/4 cup flour
2 packages chicken or
    vegetable ramen,
    crushed and with
    seasoning packets
1 teaspoon curry
    powder
3 (12-ounce) cans
    evaporated milk
2 cups water
2 cups chicken broth
3 cups cubed cooked
    chicken

In a large saucepan, sauté carrots, celery, and onion in butter until tender. Stir in the flour, seasoning packets, and curry until smooth. Gradually add milk. Bring to a boil, stirring regularly until thickened. Gradually add water and broth. Return to a boil and add chicken and noodles. Continue to boil for 3 minutes. Remove from heat and serve.

Chicken Chile Ramen

Makes 4–6 servings

3 tablespoons peanut oil
3 shallots, sliced
2 teaspoons minced garlic
1/4 teaspoon ground ginger
1 carrot, diced
1 mild green chile, diced
6 cups water
2 tablespoons soy sauce
2 packages chicken ramen noodles, with seasoning packets
2 chicken breasts, cooked and diced

Heat oil in a large frying pan over medium high heat. Once oil is warm, add shallots and stir. Add the garlic, ginger, carrot, and chile and stir. When the vegetables have softened slightly, add water, soy sauce, and seasoning packets. Mix and allow to simmer for 5–10 minutes. Add noodles and chicken and allow to cook another 3 minutes.

Beefed-Up Noodles

Makes 2 servings

2 cups water
1/8 cup diced onion
1/8 cup sliced carrots
1/8 cup diced celery
1 sprig parsley
1 small bay leaf
1/8 teaspoon thyme
   leaves
1 package beef ramen
   noodles, with
   seasoning packet

In a medium saucepan, heat all ingredients except noodles and seasoning packet to boiling. Add seasoning packet. Reduce heat and simmer 30 minutes. Strain liquid into a separate container. Add noodles to liquid and cook 3 minutes, or until noodles are done.

Vegetable Beef Noodle Soup

Makes 2—4 servings

3/4 pound ground beef
1 cup chopped tomatoes
1/2 cup chopped carrots
1/2 cup chopped celery
4 cups water
2 packages beef ramen
   noodles, with
   seasoning packets

In a large frying pan, brown and drain beef. Add vegetables, water, and seasoning packets. Bring to a boil and simmer 20 minutes. Add noodles and cook 3 minutes more, or until noodles are done.

Asian Beef-Noodle Soup

Makes 4–6 servings

1 pound ground beef,
   browned and drained
1 medium onion,
   chopped
1 tablespoon minced
   garlic
1 teaspoon ground
   ginger
5 cups water
1 medium head bok
   choy*
2 packages beef ramen
   noodles, with
   seasoning packets
1 1/2 teaspoons canola oil
2 tablespoons soy sauce

In a 4-quart soup pan, combine cooked beef, onion, garlic, ginger, and water, and bring to a boil. Stir in bok choy. Simmer over medium heat 3 minutes. Break noodles in half and stir into soup. Simmer 3–5 minutes more, or until noodles are done. Stir in seasoning packets, oil, and soy sauce.

*To prepare bok choy for use, rinse with cold water, cut off the very bottom of the stems and discard. Cut remaining bok choy into bite-size pieces.

Ham and Black-Eyed Peas

Makes 4–6 *servings*

1 tablespoon vegetable
oil
2 cups chopped collard
greens
¼ cup chopped green
onions, divided
1 clove garlic, chopped
6 cups water
2 packages pork ramen
noodles, with
seasoning packets
1 cup diced ham
1 (15-ounce) can black-
eyed peas, drained
and rinsed
2 tablespoons chopped
cilantro

Add oil to a large saucepan over medium-high heat. When the oil is warm, add collard greens, half of the onions, and garlic. Stir-fry for 2 minutes. Don't overcook; the collards should still be bright green. Add water and seasoning packets and bring to a boil. Add noodles, ham, and black-eyed peas. Allow to simmer for 3 minutes. Portion and garnish with reserved onion and cilantro.

Tuna Noodle Stew

Makes 2–4 servings

3 cups water
1 package shrimp ramen noodles, with seasoning packet
1 teaspoon vinegar
1/2 teaspoon lemon juice
Dash hot sauce
Pinch dill weed
2 teaspoons dried onion flakes
1 (6-ounce) can tuna, drained

In a medium saucepan, bring water to a boil over medium heat. Add the seasoning packet, vinegar, lemon juice, hot sauce, dill weed, and onion flakes. Allow to simmer for 3 minutes. Add tuna and noodles and cook another 3 minutes.

Spicy Shrimp and Noodle Soup

Makes 6–8 *servings*

1 tablespoon lemon juice
1/4 teaspoon chili powder
1/4 teaspoon ground
   cumin
1/8 teaspoon pepper
1 pound ready-to-cook
   shrimp
6 cups water
2 packages oriental
   ramen noodles, with
   seasoning packets
2 cups salsa
1 (15-ounce) can black
   beans, rinsed and
   drained
1 (15-ounce) can corn,
   drained
1 green onion, sliced

In a medium bowl, combine lemon juice, chili powder, cumin, and pepper; add shrimp and toss to coat. Let stand 20 minutes.

In a large saucepan bring the water and seasoning packets to boil. Add noodles, shrimp, salsa, beans, corn, and onion heat though until shrimp turn pink, about 3 minutes.

Mexican Ramen Soup

Makes 2–4 servings

3 cups water
1 lime, juiced
4 tablespoons chili powder
1 teaspoon garlic powder
Dash hot sauce
1/4 teaspoon chopped cilantro
2 packages chicken ramen noodles, with seasoning packets
1 chicken breast, cooked and cubed
1 (16-ounce) can corn, drained
1 (16-ounce) can black beans, drained and rinsed
1 medium avocado, diced
1/4 cup sour cream
Tortilla chips, crushed

In a large saucepan add water, lime juice, chili powder, garlic, hot sauce, cilantro, and seasoning packets. Bring to a boil over medium heat. Add noodles, chicken, corn, and beans. Allow to cook for 3 minutes. Portion into bowls and top with avocado, sour cream, and tortilla chips.

Mayan Soup

Makes 4–6 servings

6 cups water
**2 packages chicken
ramen noodles, with
seasoning packets**
1 lime, juiced
1/8 teaspoon pepper
**1 teaspoon chopped
parsley**
2 green onions, chopped

Bring water, seasoning packets, lime juice, pepper, parsley, and onions to a boil in large saucepan over high heat. Add noodles and cook for 3 minutes.

Egg Drop Soup

Makes 2 servings

2 cups water
2 eggs, beaten
1/4 cup diced onion
1/4 cup diced celery
**1/4 cup diced green bell
pepper**
**1 package chicken
ramen noodles, with
seasoning packet**

In a medium saucepan, bring water to boiling and add seasoning packet, eggs, and vegetables. Stir constantly until eggs look done. Simmer 5 minutes. Add noodles and cook 3–5 minutes more, or until noodles are tender.

Asian Ramen Noodle Soup

Makes 4–6 servings

6 cups water

2 packages chicken ramen noodles, with seasoning packets

4 ounces cooked boneless pork loin, sliced

3/4 cup thinly sliced mushrooms

1/2 cup cubed firm tofu

3 tablespoons white vinegar

3 tablespoons sherry

1 tablespoon soy sauce

1/2 teaspoon ground red pepper

1 egg, beaten

1/4 cup chopped green onions

Bring the water and both seasoning packets to a boil in large saucepan over high heat; add pork, mushrooms, and tofu. Reduce heat to medium-low; simmer, covered, 5 minutes. Stir in vinegar, sherry, soy sauce, and red pepper. Return broth mixture to a boil over high heat and add noodles, add more water to ensure noodles are covered. Cook for 3 minutes. Slowly stir in egg and onions.

Miso Ramen

2 teaspoons olive oil
1 teaspoon minced fresh
  ginger
1 clove garlic, minced
2 ounces ground pork
2 carrots, cut into thin
  strips
1 cup bean sprouts,
  rinsed
1 cup chopped cabbage
4 cups water
2 packages chicken
  ramen noodles, with
  seasoning packets
1 teaspoon sugar
2 teaspoons light soy
  sauce
4 tablespoons miso
1/2 teaspoon sesame oil

Heat olive oil in a large saucepan or a wok and cook the ginger, garlic, and pork on medium heat until pork is no longer pink. Add carrots, sprouts, and cabbage and sauté for 2 minutes, stirring. Add the water, seasoning packets, sugar, and soy sauce; mix and bring to a boil. Add noodles and allow to simmer for 3 minutes. Turn heat down to low and melt miso in the soup. Add sesame oil and remove from heat.

Salads

Pasta Salad

Makes 2 servings

1 package ramen
    noodles, any flavor,
    with seasoning
    packet
$1/2$ cup mayonnaise
1 tablespoon mustard
$1^{1}/_{2}$ teaspoons honey
1 celery stalk, chopped
$1/_{4}$ cup cubed cheddar
    cheese
2 hard-boiled eggs,
    chopped

Cook noodles in water according to package directions and drain. Mix mayonnaise, mustard, and honey with $1/2$ of the seasoning packet. Add noodles, celery, cheese, and eggs. Toss gently to coat.

Spring Salad

2 packages chicken
  ramen noodles, with
  seasoning packets
2 teaspoons sesame oil
3 tablespoons lemon
  juice
1/3 cup vegetable oil
2 teaspoons sugar
1 cup halved red and/
  or green seedless
  grapes
1/2 cup diced red and/or
  green apple
1/2 cup diced pineapple
  chunks
3 tablespoons chopped
  green onion
8 ounces smoked turkey
  breast, cut in strips
1/4 cup walnut pieces

Cook noodles in water according
to package directions and drain.
Rinse with cold water. Add sesame
oil and refrigerate.

For dressing, combine lemon juice,
vegetable oil, seasoning packets,
and sugar. Pour over noodles then
add remaining ingredients. Toss
to coat.

Summer Picnic Salad

Makes 2 servings

1 package ramen
   noodles, any flavor,
   broken up
1/4 cup alfalfa sprouts
1/2 cup peas
French dressing

Cook noodles in water according to package directions and drain. Top with alfalfa sprouts and peas. Mix with desired amount of dressing.

Nutty Grape Salad

Makes 6–8 servings

1 head romaine lettuce,
   chopped into bite-
   size pieces
20 purple grapes, halved
3 green onions, sliced
1 1/2 cups raspberry
   vinaigrette
1 package ramen
   noodles, any flavor,
   crushed
1/2 cup chopped walnuts

In a large bowl, toss together the lettuce, grapes, and onions. Add vinaigrette and toss to coat. Add noodles and walnuts; toss again and serve.

Mandarin Salad

Makes 6–8 servings

2 packages ramen
noodles, any flavor,
crushed

1 cup peanuts, chopped

1 (16-ounce) package
coleslaw mix

1 bunch green onions,
sliced

1 small red bell pepper,
sliced

1 (15-ounce) can
mandarin orange
segments, drained

1/2 cup sugar

1/2 cup vegetable oil

1/4 cup cider vinegar

1 tablespoon soy sauce

Preheat oven to 350 degrees.

Place the noodles and peanuts on a baking sheet and toast until golden brown; about 15 minutes. Remove from pan and allow to cool.

In a large bowl, combine coleslaw, onions, bell pepper, oranges, noodles, and peanuts; toss. In a small bowl, mix the sugar, oil, vinegar, and soy sauce until well combined. Pour over the salad and toss to coat.

Fruity Ramen Salad

Makes 2 servings

Dressing:

1/2 teaspoon salt
Dash pepper
1 teaspoon vegetable oil
1 tablespoon chopped
    parsley
2 tablespoons sugar
2 tablespoons vinegar
Dash Tabasco

Salad:

1 package ramen
    noodles, any flavor
1/2 cup slivered almonds
2 tablespoons sugar
1 cup diced fully-cooked
    ham
1 small can mandarin
    oranges, drained

In a small bowl, combine dressing ingredients and set aside. Cook noodles in water according to package directions, and then drain and rinse noodles with cold water.

In a small frying pan, lightly brown almonds and sugar over medium heat, stirring constantly so almonds are coated in sugar. In a medium bowl, mix ham, oranges, and noodles. Add dressing and toss to coat. Just before serving, add almonds and toss again.

Fruit Salad

Makes 4–6 servings

2 large oranges, peeled and diced
1 large pear, diced
1 large apple, diced
5 tablespoons brown sugar
1 package ramen noodles, any flavor, crushed

In a large bowl, combine the fruit and brown sugar. Mix well and allow it to sit for 5 minutes; toss. Just before serving, add crushed noodles and toss again.

Antipasto Salad

Makes 2–4 servings

2 packages ramen noodles, any flavor
3/4 cup cubed pepperoni
1/2 cup sliced black olives
1/4 cup sliced onion
Italian dressing

Cook noodles in water according to package directions and drain. Add pepperoni, olives, and onion. Drizzle desired amount of dressing over top and toss to coat.

Zucchini Salad

1 package ramen noodles, any flavor
1/2 cup chopped zucchini
1/2 cup chopped carrots
1/8 cup sliced olives
1 teaspoon Dijon mustard
1/2 teaspoon basil
1/4 teaspoon oregano
1/4 teaspoon garlic powder
2 tablespoons vinegar

Cook noodles in water according to package directions and drain. Add vegetables to noodles. Mix together mustard, spices, and vinegar. Add to noodle mixture and toss to coat.

Broccoli Slaw

Makes 6 servings

2/3 cup vegetable oil
1/3 cup white vinegar
1/4 cup sugar
1 package chicken
    ramen noodles,
    crushed and with
    seasoning packet
1 (16-ounce) package
    broccoli coleslaw
2 bunches green onions,
    thinly sliced
3/4 cup dried cranberries
1/2 cup sliced almonds
1/2 cup sunflower seeds

In a small bowl, combine oil, vinegar, sugar, and seasoning packet to make the dressing. Mix until sugar dissolves and chill for at least 30 minutes.

Combine broccoli coleslaw, onions, and cranberries in a large bowl. In a medium bowl, combine the almonds, noodles, and sunflower seeds. When ready to serve, combine all ingredients together and toss.

Cole Slaw

1 package chicken
   ramen noodles, finely
   crushed and with
   seasoning packet
1/4 cup apple cider
   vinegar
1/4 cup sugar
1/2 teaspoon salt
1/4 teaspoon black
   pepper
3 tablespoons canola oil
2 teaspoons sesame oil
1 (16-ounce) package
   coleslaw mix
6 green onions, thinly
   sliced
1 cup sliced almonds,
   toasted
1/2 teaspoon celery seed

In medium bowl, add noodles, seasoning packet, vinegar, sugar, salt, and pepper. Stir to mix well. Add oils and stir well to make the dressing. Allow to sit at least 5 minutes but no more than 10 minutes. In large bowl, add slaw mix, onions, almonds, and celery seed. Toss to mix. Add noodle dressing and toss to coat. Portion and serve.

Three-Bean Salad

Makes 2 servings

**1 package ramen
    noodles, any flavor**
¹/₂ cup green beans
**¹/₂ cup canned kidney
    beans, rinsed and
    drained**
**¹/₂ cup canned lima
    beans, rinsed and
    drained**
¹/₄ cup Italian dressing
Salt and pepper, to taste

Cook noodles in water according to package directions and drain. In a medium bowl, combine the noodles and beans and stir in dressing. Season with salt and pepper.

Taco Salad

Makes 2–4 servings

2 packages beef ramen noodles, with seasoning packets
1 pound ground beef, browned and drained
1 large tomato, chopped
³/₄ cup chopped onion
2 cups grated cheddar cheese
Thousand Island dressing or salsa

Cook noodles in water according to package directions and drain. In a medium bowl, stir 1 seasoning packet into cooked beef. Add tomato, onion, and cheese. Spoon mixture over warm noodles and drizzle with dressing or salsa.

Quick Chicken Salad

Makes 6–8 servings

2 boneless chicken
   breast halves, cooked
   and diced
$1/2$ cup almonds
2 green onions, sliced
1 tablespoon sugar
2 tablespoons sesame
   seeds
1 package chicken
   ramen noodles,
   crushed and with
   seasoning packet
$1/2$ medium head lettuce,
   shredded
$1/2$ cup vegetable oil
3 tablespoons distilled
   white vinegar

In a large bowl, combine the chicken, almonds, onions, sugar, sesame seeds, noodles, and lettuce.

In a small bowl, combine the oil, seasoning packet, and vinegar. Pour dressing over salad and toss to coat. Let stand overnight in refrigerator.

Oriental Chicken Salad

Makes 6 servings

³/₄ cup plus 3 tablespoons vegetable oil, divided
4¹/₂ tablespoons seasoned rice vinegar
4¹/₂ tablespoons sugar
2 packages oriental ramen noodles, finely crushed and with seasoning packets
1 cup slivered almonds
1 head cabbage, shredded
1 bunch green onions, finely chopped
2 cups cooked and diced chicken breasts
3 tablespoons sunflower seeds

In a small bowl, mix ³/₄ cup oil, vinegar, sugar, and 1 seasoning packet to make the dressing.

In a medium frying pan, add remaining oil and noodles. Cook over medium heat until lightly brown. Add almonds and continue to cook until almonds are toasted. Remove from pan and set aside.

Combine cabbage, onions, chicken, and sunflower seeds in a large bowl. Add the noodle mixture and toss. Add dressing and toss to coat.

Tangerine Chicken Salad

Makes 6–8 *servings*

1 (15-ounce) can
   tangerines or
   mandarin oranges,
   juice reserved
$1/4$ cup cider vinegar
2 tablespoons sugar
2 tablespoons soy sauce
2 teaspoons plus 1
   tablespoon sesame
   oil, divided
2 packages chicken
   ramen noodles,
   crushed
2 tablespoons sesame
   seeds
$1/2$ cup slivered almonds
$1/2$ head red or green
   cabbage, sliced
1 cup shredded carrots
1 bunch green onions,
   chopped
1 head lettuce, sliced
1 chicken breast,
   cooked and finely
   diced

Preheat the oven to 350 degrees.

In a small bowl, whisk together the reserved juice, vinegar, sugar, soy sauce, and 2 teaspoons sesame oil to make the dressing; set aside. In a medium bowl, toss the noodles, sesame seeds, almonds, and remaining sesame oil. Spread the mixture onto a baking sheet and bake for 10 minutes. Stir and bake 5 minutes more, or until the noodles are golden brown. Allow to cool completely.

In a large serving bowl, combine the cabbage, carrots, onions, and lettuce. Add the toasted noodle mixture, tangerines, chicken, and dressing; toss to coat.

Chicken Fajita Ramen Salad

Makes 6–8 servings

1 package spicy ramen
noodles, crushed
and with seasoning
packet

2 boneless chicken
breasts

3 tablespoons vegetable
oil, divided

1 small onion, sliced

1 small red bell pepper,
sliced

1 small green bell
pepper, sliced

1 large tomato, diced

2 limes, juiced

1 teaspoon dried
cilantro

2 tablespoons soy sauce

1/2 tablespoon cayenne
pepper

1 teaspoon sugar

Lightly sprinkle seasoning packet on both sides of chicken breasts (using about 1/4 of the packet in all). Place 2 tablespoons oil in a large frying pan over medium heat. Brown each side of chicken breasts, then cover and cook until done. Cut into strips and place in a large bowl. Sauté the onion and bell peppers in the pan until tender. Add to chicken, along with noodles and tomato; toss to mix.

In a small bowl, whisk together the lime juice, cilantro, soy sauce, cayenne pepper, sugar, remaining oil, and remaining seasoning from packet. Drizzle over chicken mixture and toss. Can be served immediately or chilled and served cold.

Asian Chicken Salad

Makes 2–4 servings

1 package ramen
    noodles, any flavor
1 cup slivered almonds
1 teaspoon vinegar
1/2 cup oil
3 teaspoons seasoned
    salt
1/2 teaspoon pepper
3 tablespoons sugar
4 cups shredded cooked
    chicken breast
3–6 green onions, sliced
3/4 cup sliced celery
1/4 cup sesame seeds
1/2 head lettuce, torn or
    shredded

Preheat oven to 350 degrees.

Roast almonds in oven until lightly browned; about 10–12 minutes.

Cook noodles in water according to package directions for 1 minute and drain.

In a large bowl, mix vinegar, oil, salt, pepper, and sugar. Add chicken, onions, celery, and sesame seeds. Add lettuce, noodles, and almonds just before serving and toss.

Tofu Salad

2 cups cubed tofu
2 tablespoons soy sauce
¼ teaspoon garlic
powder
¼ teaspoon onion
powder
2 tablespoons sugar
3 tablespoons white
vinegar
⅛ cup, plus 1 tablespoon
sesame oil, divided
⅛ cup olive oil
1 package ramen
noodles, any flavor,
crushed
3 tablespoons sesame
seeds
¼ cup slivered almonds
4 green onions, thinly
sliced
1 red bell pepper, diced
½ head cabbage,
shredded

Preheat the oven to 350 degrees.

Place tofu on several paper towels, cover with another paper towel, and press to remove liquid.

In a small bowl, whisk the soy sauce, garlic powder, onion powder, sugar, vinegar, ⅛ cup sesame oil, and olive oil. Place in a ziplock bag and add tofu. Flip to distribute marinade. Allow to sit 5 minutes, shaking regularly.

In a small bowl, add crushed noodles, sesame seeds, almonds, and remaining sesame oil; toss to coat. Spread the mixture onto a baking sheet and bake for 10 minutes. Stir and bake 5 minutes more, or until the noodles are golden brown. Allow to cool completely.

In a large bowl, combine the onions, bell pepper, and cabbage. Add toasted mixture and tofu with marinade; toss to coat.

Oriental Salad

1/2 cup oil
1/4 cup apple cider
    vinegar
2 tablespoons sugar
2 packages oriental
    ramen noodles,
    crushed with
    seasoning packets
1/3 cup sliced almonds
1/4 cup sesame seeds
2 tablespoons butter or
    margarine, melted
1 head green cabbage,
    shredded
1 red bell pepper, thinly
    sliced
1 orange bell pepper,
    thinly sliced
1 cup snow peas
4 green onions, thinly
    sliced

In a medium bowl, whisk the oil, vinegar, sugar, and 1 seasoning packet to make dressing; set aside.

In a medium bowl, combine almonds, sesame seeds, noodles, and butter; toss to coat. Transfer to a frying pan and cook over medium heat until almonds are toasted. Do not burn. Remove from pan and set aside.

In a large bowl, combine the cabbage, bell peppers, snow peas, and onions; toss. Just before serving, combine the toasted mixture with the cabbage and toss. Pour the dressing over salad and toss to coat.

Water Chestnut Ramen Salad

Makes 4–6 *servings*

4 packages chicken ramen noodles, with seasoning packets
1 cup diced celery
1 (8-ounce) can sliced water chestnuts, drained
1 cup chopped red onion
1 cup diced green bell pepper
1 cup peas
1 cup mayonnaise

Break each package of noodles into 4 pieces. Cook noodles in water according to package directions, and then drain and rinse noodles with cold water.

In a large bowl, stir noodles, celery, water chestnuts, onion, pepper, and peas together. Combine mayonnaise and 3 of the 4 seasoning packets. Fold mayonnaise mixture into salad. Cover and refrigerate at least 1 hour before serving.

Sweet-and-Sour Salad

Makes 6–8 *servings*

1 cup canola or olive oil
¹/₂ cup sugar
¹/₂ cup cider vinegar
1 tablespoon soy sauce
¹/₂ cup butter
1 cup chopped walnuts
1 package ramen
noodles, any flavor,
crushed
1 head romaine lettuce
4 cups chopped fresh
broccoli
¹/₂ cup chopped green
onions

Combine oil, sugar, vinegar, and soy sauce together in a small bowl and refrigerate overnight.

In a small saucepan, melt butter over medium heat. Stir walnuts and noodles into butter. Stir until heated.

Tear lettuce into bite-size pieces and place in a large bowl. Add broccoli and onions. Pour dressing over top and toss to coat. Sprinkle walnuts and ramen mixture over salad.

Sprouting Ramen Salad

Makes 4–6 servings

6 cups water
2 packages ramen noodles, any flavor
2/3 cup alfalfa sprouts
3 tablespoons sesame seeds
1/4 cup red wine vinegar
2 tablespoons soy sauce
2 tablespoons sesame oil
1 1/2 tablespoons sugar
1 teaspoon Chinese red chili sauce
1/3 cup sliced green onions
2 tablespoons minced fresh gingerroot
2 cups bean sprouts
1/2 cup radish sprouts

In a large saucepan, bring water to a boil. Add noodles and cook for 3 minutes; drain and set aside. Pull alfalfa sprouts apart; set aside.

In a small ungreased frying pan over high heat, toast the sesame seeds until golden, about 4 minutes. Remove from pan and set aside.

Combine the vinegar, soy sauce, sesame oil, sugar, chili sauce, onions, and ginger. Mix well and add to noodles; toss to coat and refrigerate for at least 1 hour.

Toss noodles with sprouts and seeds.

Polish Ramen Salad

Makes 6–8 *servings*

3 teaspoons mayonnaise

1 cup plain yogurt

2 teaspoons paprika

3 packages chicken
ramen noodles,
crushed and with
seasoning packets

2 tomatoes, diced

1 cucumber, diced

1 (15-ounce) can corn,
drained

1 (12.5-ounce) can
kidney beans, rinsed
and drained

In a large bowl, whisk the mayonnaise, yogurt, paprika, and 1 seasoning packet. Add noodles and toss to coat. Add the tomatoes, cucumber, corn, and beans. Toss to coat and refrigerate for at least 1 hour.

Beef & Pork Dishes

Meatballs and Pineapple Ramen

Makes 4–6 *servings*

4 cups water
2 packages beef ramen
    noodles, with
    seasoning packets
1/2 pound ground beef
2 teaspoons garlic
    powder
1/3 cup vegetable oil
1 (8-ounce) can
    pineapple chunks,
    drained
1 red bell pepper, sliced

In a large saucepan, bring water to a boil. Add noodles and cook for 3 minutes; drain and set aside.

In a medium bowl, mix the ground beef, seasoning packets, and garlic powder. Form into small meatballs. In a large frying pan, heat oil over medium heat. Add the meatballs and brown on all sides. Reduce the heat and allow to simmer for 10 minutes. Add pineapple and bell pepper and continue to cook for 5 minutes more. Add noodles to pan; toss and serve.

Ramen Rolled Steak

Makes 6–8 *servings*

1¹/₂ pounds flank steaks
1 package beef ramen
    noodles, crushed,
    with seasoning
    packet
Pepper, to taste
1 egg
1 tablespoon water
1 tablespoon flour
2 tablespoons steak
    sauce

Preheat oven to 350 degrees.

Pound 2 long pieces of flank steak on a board. Sprinkle seasoning packet and pepper on both sides of the steaks and rub in.

In small bowl, beat the egg and water. Whisk in flour until there are no lumps. Spread the mixture on one side of each of the pounded steaks. Sprinkle evenly with the crushed noodles. Roll up and pin with at least 4 toothpicks in each roll. Place each roll in a mini loaf pan or place rolls in a baking dish that has been prepared with non-stick cooking spray. Bake for 30–35 minutes, uncovered. Rub rolled steak with steak sauce. Bake for 10 minutes more. Let cool for about 10 minutes before cutting. Slice between toothpicks and serve.

Yatsobi

1 pound lean ground
   beef
6 slices bacon
1 medium red onion,
   diced
3 tablespoons minced
   garlic
3 tablespoons soy sauce
3 carrots, cut into thin
   strips
1 medium cabbage,
   chopped
1 red bell pepper, diced
4 cups water
2 packages ramen
   noodles, any flavor
Splash olive oil
3 cups bean sprouts

In a large frying pan, brown the
ground beef; drain and set aside. In
the same pan, fry the bacon until
crispy; drain on paper towels and
reserve 2 tablespoons of the bacon
fat. Stir the onion and garlic into
the fat and cook for 3–4 minutes
or until onions are soft. Add the
soy sauce and carrots and cook
for 2–3 minutes. Add cabbage
and bell pepper and stir-fry on
medium heat for 5–6 minutes, or
until vegetables are tender-crisp.
Add ground beef and bacon to the
vegetable mixture and cook on
medium heat for 2–3 minutes, or
until meat is heated through.

In a large saucepan, bring water to
a boil. Add noodles and cook for 3
minutes; drain and toss with olive
oil to keep from sticking together.
Add to meat and vegetable mixture with bean sprouts and cook
for 3 minutes, stirring frequently.

Crock-Pot Beef and Noodles

Makes 10–14 servings

2 pounds beef roast
14 cups water, divided
6 packages beef ramen
    noodles, with
    seasoning packets
2 large white onions,
    diced

Place roast in a 4-quart crock-pot with 1 cup water on low heat and allow to cook overnight or for 8–9 hours. Shred the meat and add all seasoning packets, onion, and 1 cup water. Allow to cook, on low, another 1–2 hours.

About 15 minutes before serving, bring remaining water to a boil in a large saucepan. Add noodles and cook for 3 minutes. Drain, place in a large serving bowl, and mix in the beef.

Stuffed Bell Peppers

Makes 6 servings

3 green bell peppers
1 (14.5-ounce) can diced tomatoes, divided
1 (8-ounce) can tomato sauce, divided
1 tablespoon olive oil
1 small onion, diced
4 tablespoons minced garlic
1 pound ground beef
1 package beef ramen noodles, finely crushed, and with seasoning packet
1/2 cup grated Monterey Jack cheese

Preheat oven to 375 degrees.

Cut bell peppers in half, crosswise. Remove seeds and place on paper towels to drain.

In a medium mixing bowl, combine a third of the tomatoes and half the tomato sauce and set aside.

Add the olive oil to a large frying pan. Heat on medium low and add the onion and garlic. Sauté for 4–5 minutes or until soft. Add the beef and seasoning packet, mix well, and continue to cook until beef has browned. Remove from heat. Add the noodles, remaining tomatoes, and remaining tomato sauce; mix well.

Place the bell peppers as bowls in a 9 x 13-inch glass casserole dish and fill with beef mixture. Top with the tomato sauce mixture. Cover with foil and bake for about 1 hour, or until peppers are tender. Uncover and bake 10 minutes more. Sprinkle with cheese and bake for 5 minutes.

Beef Ramenoff

Makes 2 servings

1/2 pound beef strips
2 cups sour cream
**1 tablespoon chopped
   chives**
1 teaspoon salt
1/8 teaspoon pepper
1 garlic clove, crushed
**1/2 cup grated Parmesan
   cheese, divided**
**1 package ramen
   noodles, any flavor**
**2 tablespoons butter or
   margarine**

In a large frying pan, brown beef until done. Add sour cream, spices, and 1/4 cup Parmesan and simmer over low heat.

Cook noodles in water according to package directions and drain. Stir butter into warm noodles until melted. Fold in beef mixture. Sprinkle with reserved cheese.

Creamy Beef and Broccoli Noodles

Makes 2 servings

- ¾ **pound beef sirloin, cubed**
- ½ **teaspoon garlic powder**
- 1 **onion, cut in wedges**
- 2 **cups broccoli pieces**
- 1 **(10.75-ounce) can cream of broccoli soup, condensed**
- ¼ **cup water**
- 1 **tablespoon soy sauce**
- 2 **packages beef ramen noodles, with seasoning packets**

In a large frying pan, brown beef with garlic powder until done. Stir in onion and broccoli. Cook over medium heat until vegetables are tender. Add soup, water, and soy sauce. Simmer 10 minutes.

Cook noodles in water according to package directions and drain. Add seasoning packets. Serve beef mixture over warm noodles.

Marinated Beef

Makes 2 servings

- 3/4 pound beef strips
- 1 package beef ramen noodles, with seasoning packet
- 1/2 cup water
- 2 tablespoons oil
- 1/4 cup sliced green onion
- 1 tablespoon butter or margarine
- 1 (14.5-ounce) can diced tomatoes, drained

Marinate beef in seasoning packet, water, and oil for 30 minutes. In a large frying pan, cook beef in marinade until done. Add onion and butter, and sauté 5 minutes.

Cook noodles in water according to package directions and drain. Add tomatoes and cooked noodles to beef mixture. Simmer 5–10 minutes, or until heated through.

Beef Provencale

Makes 2 servings

1 pound beef strips
2 tablespoons butter or
margarine
1 onion, sliced
2 tablespoons flour
1 cup water mixed with
seasoning packet
1 tomato, chopped
1 (4-ounce) can sliced
mushrooms, drained
1 teaspoon garlic
powder
1 package beef ramen
noodles, with
seasoning packet

In a large frying pan, brown beef until done; drain and set aside.

In a large saucepan, heat butter until golden brown. Add onion and cook until tender, then discard onion. Stir in flour, over low heat, until it is brown. Remove from heat. Add water mixture and heat to boiling, stirring constantly for 1 minute. Gently stir in tomato, mushrooms, and garlic powder.

Cook noodles in water according to package directions and drain. Top warm noodles with beef and sauce.

Cheddar Beef Casserole

Makes 2–4 servings

2 packages beef ramen
   noodles, with
   seasoning packets
1 pound ground beef
$1/2$ cup sliced celery
$1/4$ cup chopped green
   bell pepper
$1/2$ cup chopped onion
3 cups grated cheddar
   cheese
2 cups corn
1 (6-ounce) can tomato
   paste
$1/2$ cup water

Preheat oven to 350 degrees.

Cook noodles in water according to package directions; drain and set aside.

In a large frying pan, brown beef with celery, pepper, and onion; drain and set aside. In a 2-quart casserole dish, mix remaining ingredients with 1 seasoning packet. Add beef mixture and noodles. Bake 15–20 minutes.

Beef and Broccoli Stir-Fry

Makes 2—4 servings

1 pound beef steak strips
1 tablespoon oil
2 cups broccoli pieces
1 cup green onions, cut in strips
2 tablespoons soy sauce
1/4 teaspoon crushed red pepper
2 packages beef ramen noodles, with seasoning packets

In a large frying pan, brown beef until done; drain. Add oil, 1 seasoning packet, broccoli, and onions. Stir-fry 5 minutes. Add soy sauce and red pepper. Simmer 5 minutes more.

Cook noodles in water according to package directions and drain. Serve beef mixture over warm noodles.

Beefy Mushroom Noodles

Makes 2–4 servings

2 packages beef ramen noodles, with seasoning packets
1 1/2 pounds beef strips
1/4 cup butter or margarine
2 (4-ounce) cans sliced mushrooms, drained
1/4 cup flour
2 cups water mixed with seasoning packets
Worcestershire sauce

Cook noodles in water according to package directions and drain.

In a large frying pan, brown beef until done; drain.

In a small saucepan, melt butter over low heat. Stir in mushrooms and brown slowly. Add flour and cook, stirring, until deep brown. Add water mixture. Heat to boiling and stir 1 minute. Add Worcestershire sauce to taste. Top warm noodles with beef and sauce.

Beef Sukiyaki

Makes 2–4 servings

1 pound stir-fry beef
2 tablespoons oil
$^1/_2$ cup water mixed with
    half of seasoning
    packet
2 tablespoons sugar
$^1/_2$ cup soy sauce
1 (4-ounce) can sliced
    mushrooms, drained
$^1/_2$ cup sliced green
    onions
1 cup sliced onion
1 celery stalk, sliced
1 small can bamboo
    shoots
3 cups fresh spinach
2 packages beef ramen
    noodles, with
    seasoning packets

In a large frying pan, brown beef in oil until done, and then push to one side of the pan. Stir in water, sugar, and soy sauce. Add remaining ingredients except noodles and cook until tender. Cover and simmer 5 minutes. Stir together.

Cook noodles in water according to package directions and drain. Add seasoning packets. Serve beef mixture over warm noodles.

Vegetable Beef Noodles

Makes 2 servings

½ pound ground beef
**1 (8-ounce) can tomato
  sauce**
**2 cups frozen mixed
  vegetables**
**1 package beef ramen
  noodles, with
  seasoning packet**

In a large frying pan, brown beef until done; drain. Add tomato sauce, seasoning packet, and vegetables to cooked beef. Simmer 10 minutes, or until vegetables are tender.

Cook noodles in water according to package directions and drain. Add noodles to beef mixture and simmer 2–3 minutes.

Beef 'n' Potato Noodles

Makes 2–4 servings

1 pound ground beef
2 cups cubed potatoes
2 cups diced tomatoes
**2 packages beef ramen
  noodles, with
  seasoning packets**

In a large frying pan, brown beef with seasoning packets until done. Add potatoes and cook until tender.

Cook noodles in water according to package directions and drain. Stir in tomatoes, then add noodles and tomatoes to beef mixture and simmer 5 minutes.

Beefy Chili Noodles

Makes 2–4 servings

1 pound ground beef
2 packages beef ramen noodles, with seasoning packets
2 (4-ounce) cans sliced mushrooms, drained
1/2 cup chopped onion
1/2 cup chopped tomato
1 (15-ounce) can kidney beans, rinsed and drained
1/4 teaspoon chili powder
1 cup water

In a large frying pan, brown beef until done; drain. Add remaining ingredients and 1 seasoning packet. Simmer 10 minutes over medium heat or until noodles are done.

Ramen Burgers

Makes 4 hamburgers

1 package beef ramen
   noodles, with
   seasoning packet
1 pound ground beef
1 egg
Hamburger buns
Condiments

Cook noodles $1\frac{1}{2}$ minutes and drain. Add beef, egg, and $\frac{1}{2}$ of the seasoning packet. Mix well and form into four patties. Grill or cook 5 minutes per side, or until done. Serve with the usual hamburger fixings.

Cheeseburger Ramen

Makes 2 servings

$\frac{1}{2}$ pound ground beef
1 package beef ramen
   noodles, with
   seasoning packet
1 cup grated cheddar
   cheese
1 tomato, diced
   (optional)

In a medium frying pan, brown beef until done; drain. Season to taste with $\frac{1}{2}$ of the seasoning packet.

Cook noodles in water according to package directions and drain. Add beef and cheese to noodles and stir until cheese is melted. Add tomatoes, if desired.

Spicy Meat Loaf Cheese Roll

Makes 2–4 servings

1 pound ground beef
1 package beef ramen
   noodles, crushed
1 cup grated cheddar
   cheese
1/2 cup salsa

Preheat oven to 350 degrees.

Flatten beef into a 1/2-inch-thick rectangle. Sprinkle uncooked noodles over beef. Top with a layer of cheese. Roll from one end to the other and pinch ends to prevent cheese from melting to the outside. Place in a loaf pan and top with salsa. Bake 30 minutes. Top with more salsa before serving, if desired.

Spicy Beef Noodles

Makes 2–4 servings

**2 packages ramen
noodles, any flavor,
with seasoning
packets**
¹/₂ pound ground beef
**¹/₂ pound ground spicy
sausage**
¹/₂ cup diced onion
**³/₄ cup diced green bell
pepper**
³/₄ cup salsa

Cook noodles in water according
to package directions; drain and
set aside.

In a large frying pan, brown beef
and sausage together until done;
drain. Add onion, pepper, and
salsa. Cook until vegetables are
tender; add noodles and simmer
2–3 minutes.

Beefy Noodles
with Gravy

Makes 2 servings

1 pound beef strips
**1 package beef ramen
noodles, with
seasoning packet**
1 envelope brown gravy

In a medium frying pan, brown
beef until done.

Cook noodles in water according
to package directions; drain and
set aside.

In a saucepan, cook gravy according to package directions. Top
warm noodles with beef and gravy.

Ramen Noodle Casserole

Makes 4–6 servings

1 pound ground beef
2 packages beef ramen
   noodles, with
   seasoning packets
1 medium onion,
   chopped
3 cups water
1 (10.5-ounce) can
   cream of mushroom
   soup, condensed
1 (10.5-ounce) can
   cream of celery soup,
   condensed
1 (5-ounce) can sliced
   water chestnuts
$1/2$ cup milk
1 cup grated cheddar
   cheese, divided

Preheat oven to 350 degrees.

In a large frying pan, brown the ground beef with seasoning packets and onion. In a medium saucepan, bring water to a boil and add the noodles; cook for 3 minutes and then drain. When beef is browned, add noodles, soups, water chestnuts, milk, and $1/2$ cup cheese. Pour into an 8 x 8-inch glass baking dish that has been prepared with nonstick cooking spray and top with remaining cheese. Bake uncovered for 20–25 minutes.

Mexican Ramen Casserole

Makes 4–6 servings

- 1 pound ground beef
- 2 cups chunky salsa, divided
- 2 cups water
- 2 packages beef ramen noodles, with seasoning packets
- 1 (15-ounce) can corn, drained
- 1 cup grated cheddar cheese

Preheat oven to 350 degrees.

Brown the ground beef in a large saucepan; drain. Mix in 1 cup of salsa. Add water, noodles, seasoning packets, and corn and bring to a boil and cook, covered, for 3 minutes. Remove cover and simmer until water has evaporated.

Pour into an 8 x 8-inch glass baking dish that has been prepared with nonstick cooking spray and sprinkle cheese on top. Bake for 6–8 minutes, or until cheese is melted.

Layered Ramen

Makes 4–6 *servings*

1 pound ground beef
1 small onion, diced
2 packages chicken
    ramen noodles, with
    seasoning packets
1 cup grated mozzarella
    cheese, divided
1 cup grated cheddar
    cheese, divided
3 eggs
2 cups water
1 cup spaghetti sauce

Preheat oven to 325 degrees.

In large frying pan, brown the beef, onion, and 1 seasoning packet. Drain and pour into an 8 x 8-inch casserole dish that has been prepared with nonstick cooking spray. Sprinkle ¼ cup of each cheese over the beef.

Beat the eggs and cook in the same pan as the beef. Place the egg evenly over the beef and sprinkle another ¼ cup of each cheese over top.

In a small saucepan bring water to a boil. Add noodles and cook for 3 minutes; drain. Mix the spaghetti sauce into the noodles and pour on top of the eggs. Sprinkle the remaining cheese over the noodles. Bake for 10 minutes, or until cheese is melted.

Country Vegetable Beef

Makes 2–4 servings

2 cups water
2 tablespoons cornstarch
1 pound ground beef
4 cups frozen mixed vegetables
2 packages beef ramen noodles, with seasoning packets

In a small saucepan, mix water, cornstarch, and seasoning packets. Stir constantly over low heat until mixture thickens.

In a large frying pan, brown beef until done; drain. Add vegetables and cook until tender. Add gravy and stir.

Cook noodles in water according to package directions and drain. Serve beefy gravy over warm noodles.

All-American Ramen

Makes 2–4 servings

2 packages ramen noodles, any flavor, with seasoning packets
¼ cup chopped onion
4 hot dogs, sliced
1 cup grated cheddar cheese

Cook noodles in water according to package directions and drain. Add seasoning packets.

In a medium frying pan, sauté onion and hot dogs together until heated through. Add hot dog mixture to noodles. Add cheese and stir until melted.

Oriental Hot Dogs

Makes 1–2 servings

4 cups water
2 packages oriental
  ramen noodles, with
  seasoning packets
$1/4$ cup sliced yellow
  onion
1 zucchini, diagonally
  sliced
2 hot dogs, diagonally
  sliced
$1/4$ cup mustard greens
Chives, to taste

In a large saucepan, bring water to a boil. Add the seasoning packets, onion, and zucchini and reduce to medium heat. Allow to simmer for 1 minute. Add hot dogs and simmer for 1 minute. Add noodles and simmer for 2 minutes. Add mustard greens and simmer for 1 minute more. Serve topped with chives.

Ham Omelets

Makes 2-4 servings

**2 packages ramen
   noodles, any flavor,
   with seasoning
   packets**
**2 tablespoons butter or
   margarine**
6 eggs, beaten
1 cup chopped ham
$^1/_2$ cup chopped onion
**$^1/_2$ cup chopped green
   bell pepper**
**$^1/_2$–1 cup grated Swiss
   cheese**

Cook noodles in water according
to package directions and drain.
Add seasoning packets.

In a large frying pan, melt butter,
and then add beaten eggs. Fold in
noodles and remaining ingredients.
Cook until light brown.

Pork Chop Ramen

Makes 4 servings

4 pork chops
1 teaspoon oil
1/2 cup sliced onion
1 (10.75-ounce) can
cream of celery soup,
condensed
1/2 cup water
2 packages pork ramen
noodles, with
seasoning packets

In a large frying pan over medium heat, brown pork chops in oil 5 minutes per side, or until done, and drain. Add onion, soup, and water. Simmer over low heat 10 minutes.

Cook noodles in water according to package directions and drain. Add seasoning packets. Serve pork chops and sauce over warm noodles.

Cheesy Bacon Noodles

Makes 2–4 servings

2 packages ramen
noodles, any flavor
2 cups grated cheddar
cheese
1/2–1 cup bacon, cooked
and crumbled
Salt and pepper, to taste

Cook noodles in water according to package directions and drain. Add cheese immediately and stir until melted. Stir in bacon and season with salt and pepper.

Brats 'n' Noodles

Makes 2-4 servings

- **2 packages ramen noodles, any flavor, with seasoning packets**
- **4 bratwursts or cheddarwursts, sliced**

Cook noodles and brats together in a large saucepan according to package directions. Drain and stir in 1 seasoning packet.

Hungarian Skillet Meal

Makes 2 servings

- **1 package ramen noodles, any flavor**
- **1/2 pound pork strips**
- **1 (8-ounce) can tomato sauce**
- **1/4 cup onion, thinly sliced**
- **1 teaspoon paprika**
- **1/3 cup sour cream**

Cook noodles in water according to package directions and drain.

In a large frying pan, brown pork until done. Add tomato sauce, onion, paprika, and noodles. Cook over low heat until onion is tender. Stir in noodles. Remove from heat and add sour cream.

Pork and Peppers

2 pork chops

¼ cup chopped red bell pepper

¼ cup chopped green bell pepper

2 tablespoons chopped onion

1 package pork ramen noodles, with seasoning packet

2 tablespoons butter or margarine

2 tablespoons flour

1 cup water mixed with seasoning packet

1 tablespoon vinegar

¼ teaspoon tarragon leaves

¼ teaspoon thyme leaves

In a medium frying pan, brown pork chops until done and then remove. Sauté peppers and onion in drippings until tender.

Cook noodles in water according to package directions and drain.

In a small saucepan, heat butter over low heat until light brown. Add flour, stirring until deep brown. Remove from heat. Add remaining ingredients. Heat to boiling and stir 1 minute. Top warm noodles with pork chops and sauce.

Lean Pork Steak

**2 packages pork ramen
noodles, with
seasoning packets**
**2 lean pork steaks, cut
into bite-size pieces**
**1 teaspoon dried minced
onion**
3/4 cup water

Cook noodles in water according to package directions and drain.

In a large frying pan, cook steak pieces until done. Add onion, water, and seasoning packets. Simmer, covered, 10 minutes. Stir in noodles and simmer 3–5 minutes more.

Tropical Ramen

Makes 2 servings

**2 packages ramen
noodles, any flavor**
**2 cups fully-cooked
ham, cut in strips**
1 cup pineapple chunks
**1 cup crispy Chinese
noodles**
1 stalk celery, sliced

Cook noodles in water according to package directions and drain. Rinse with cold water.

Stir in ham, pineapple, crispy noodles, and celery.

Broccoli and Ham Casserole

Makes 6–8 servings

4 cups water
2 packages chicken ramen noodles, with seasoning packets
2 large heads broccoli, cut into bite-size pieces
2 cups plain yogurt
4 eggs
1 (12-ounce) package mushrooms, washed and sliced
2 cups cooked diced ham
2 cups grated mild cheddar cheese
1 medium onion, diced

Preheat oven to 350 degrees.

Prepare a 12 x 17-inch casserole dish with nonstick cooking spray.

In a medium saucepan, bring water to a boil. Add noodles and cook for 3 minutes; drain.

In a large microwave-safe bowl, add the broccoli and fill with water until broccoli is completely covered. Microwave on high for 6 minutes; drain.

In a large bowl, combine the yogurt, eggs, and seasoning packets; mix thoroughly. Add the broccoli, mushrooms, ham, cheese, onion, and noodles then toss together to evenly coat. Pour into prepared dish and bake for 1 hour, or until center is bubbly. Allow to set for 15 minutes before serving.

Gingered Pork
and Ramen

Makes 4–6 servings

**1 pound boneless pork
   shoulder, cut into
   1-inch pieces**
**2 packages chicken
   ramen noodles,
   crumbled and with
   seasoning packets**
**1 teaspoon grated
   gingerroot**
3 cups water
**1 cup halved fresh snow
   pea pods**
**1/4 cup sliced green
   onion**
1 tablespoon soy sauce
2 teaspoons cornstarch

In 3 1/2- to 4-quart crock-pot, combine the pork, seasoning packets, gingerroot and water; mix. Cover and cook on low heat for 6–8 hours.

About 30 minutes before serving, add the noodles, pea pods, and onion; mix. Turn heat setting to high; cover and cook for 10 minutes more or just until vegetables are tender-crisp.

In a small bowl, blend the soy sauce and cornstarch until smooth. Stir into pork mixture and cook for 5 minutes or until sauce is slightly thickened.

Spicy Sausage Ramen

Makes 1-2 servings

2-3 spicy Italian sausage links
¼ cup diced onion
½ cup diced green bell pepper
1 tablespoon minced garlic
2 cups water
1 package chili ramen noodles, with seasoning packet
1 (14.5-ounce) can stewed tomatoes

Poke each sausage with a fork to allow grease to escape. In a large frying pan, cook the sausage over medium heat. Remove sausage and then slice and set aside. Sauté the onion, bell pepper, and garlic in the pan with the grease from the sausage.

In a large saucepan, combine water, flavor packet, and tomatoes. Bring to a boil and add noodles, sausage, and vegetables. Cook for 3 minutes.

Pork Skillet

Makes 3–4 servings

1 tablespoon vegetable oil

¾ pound pork tenderloin, cut into strips

2 cups water

1 medium red bell pepper, cut into strips

1 cup chopped broccoli

3 medium green onions, sliced

2 teaspoons parsley flakes

1 tablespoon soy sauce

2 packages pork ramen noodles, with seasoning packets

In a large frying pan or wok over medium-high heat, add the oil, coating the entire surface.

Add pork and fry about 5 minutes or until no longer pink. Add the water, bell pepper, broccoli, onions, parsley, soy sauce, and seasoning packets. Bring to a boil and then add noodles. Boil for 3 minutes, stirring occasionally, until noodles are completely softened.

Bacon Fried Ramen

Makes 1-2 servings

4 slices raw bacon, cut in ¼-inch pieces
3 cups water
2 packages ramen noodles, any flavor
Salt and pepper, to taste
Pinch red pepper flakes
1 teaspoon soy sauce
1 egg

Place bacon into a large nonstick frying pan and let cook slowly on medium-low heat.

In a medium saucepan, bring water to a boil. Add noodles and cook for 3 minutes. Quickly drain the noodles completely and pour into a bowl of ice cold water to stop the cooking process. Stir the noodles with your hands until they are cold.

Once the bacon has finished cooking, drain the chilled noodles and combine with the bacon in the pan. Turn the stove up to medium-high heat. Season noodles and bacon with salt, pepper, red pepper flakes, and soy sauce. Continue to cook for 2-3 minutes. Move noodles to one side of the pan. Crack the egg into open side of pan, mixing the egg in the pan and let it cook for 1-2 minutes. Cut up the egg and stir in with bacon and noodles. Continue cooking and turning for 3-4 more minutes.

Breakfast Ramen

Makes 1–2 servings

2 cups water
1 package chicken
    ramen noodles
2 eggs, beaten
1/4 cup grated cheddar
    cheese
4 slices bacon, chopped
4 large mushrooms,
    diced
1 small tomato, diced

In a small saucepan, boil water. Add noodles and cook for 3 minutes; drain and place in a large bowl. Beat eggs and pour over noodles; toss. Add cheese and toss again.

In a large frying pan over medium heat, cook bacon pieces until bacon starts to crisp, stirring regularly to keep pieces separated. Add mushrooms and sauté for 1 minute. Add tomato and continue to cook until bacon is done. Add noodles and toss until evenly distributed. Cook over medium heat for 3–4 minutes stirring to ensure all the egg has been cooked completely. Noodles will begin to brown.

Chicken & Turkey Dishes

Creamy Chicken and Broccoli

Makes 2–4 servings

3 boneless, skinless chicken breasts, cut into strips

2 cups cut-up fresh or frozen broccoli

2 (10.75-ounce) cans cream of mushroom soup, condensed

1/2 cup water

2 packages chicken ramen noodles, with seasoning packets

In a large frying pan, brown chicken until done. Add broccoli and soup to chicken; cook over medium heat until broccoli is tender. Add 1/2 of 1 seasoning packet, or to taste.

Cook noodles in water according to package directions and drain. Serve chicken and broccoli mixture over warm noodles.

Spicy Chicken

3 boneless, skinless chicken breasts, cut into strips

¾ teaspoon garlic powder

1 (14.5-ounce) can diced tomatoes with green chiles, drained

1 cup chopped green bell peppers

2 cups water

2 packages chicken ramen noodles, with seasoning packets

In a large frying pan, brown chicken until done. Add garlic powder, tomatoes, peppers, water, and seasoning packets. Simmer 10 minutes. Add noodles and cook 3-5 minutes more.

Cheesy Chicken Divan

Makes 2–4 servings

2 cups fresh broccoli
   pieces
2–4 boneless, skinless
   chicken breasts, cut
   into chunks
2 packages chicken
   ramen noodles
1 (10.75-ounce) can
   cream of chicken
   soup, condensed
¾ cup mayonnaise
1 teaspoon mild curry
   powder
Salt and pepper, to taste
1 cup grated cheddar
   cheese

Preheat oven to 350 degrees.

Place broccoli in a medium saucepan and cover with water. Cook
over medium heat until broccoli is
tender; drain and spread in a lightly
greased 9 x 9-inch casserole dish.

In a large frying pan, brown
chicken until done. Spread chicken
over broccoli.

Cook noodles in water according
to package directions and drain.
Spread noodles over broccoli and
chicken.

Mix together soup, mayonnaise,
curry powder, salt, and pepper.
Spoon mixture over broccoli,
chicken, and noodles; sprinkle with
cheese and bake 30 minutes.

Chicken Hollandaise

Makes 2-4 servings

2-4 boneless, skinless chicken breasts, cut into chunks
4 egg yolks
6 tablespoons lemon juice
1 cup butter or margarine, divided
2 packages chicken ramen noodles, with seasoning packets

In a large frying pan, brown chicken until done. Season with 1/2 of 1 seasoning packet, or to taste.

In a small saucepan, whisk egg yolks and lemon juice briskly with a fork. Add 1/2 cup butter and stir over low heat until melted. Add remaining butter, stirring briskly until butter melts and sauce thickens.

Cook noodles in water according to package directions and drain. Top warm noodles with chicken and sauce.

Chicken Veloute

Makes 2 servings

1 pound boneless,
    skinless chicken
    breasts, cut into
    chunks
2 tablespoons butter or
    margarine
2 tablespoons flour
1 cup water mixed with
    seasoning packet
$\frac{1}{8}$ teaspoon nutmeg
1 package chicken
    ramen noodles, with
    seasoning packet

In a medium frying pan, brown chicken until done.

In a large saucepan, melt butter over low heat. Mix in flour, stirring until smooth and bubbly. Remove from heat. Stir in water mixture and nutmeg. Heat to boiling, stirring 1 minute. Add chicken and simmer over low heat.

Cook noodles in water according to package directions and drain. Top warm noodles with chicken and sauce.

Chicken Curry

Makes 2 servings

**2 boneless, skinless
chicken breasts**
**¼ cup butter or
margarine**
¼ cup flour
**½ teaspoon curry
powder**
2 cups milk
**2 packages chicken
ramen noodles, with
seasoning packets**

In a medium frying pan, brown chicken until done. Set aside.

In a medium saucepan, melt butter. Stir in flour, curry powder, and 1 seasoning packet. Cook on low heat, stirring until smooth and bubbly. Add milk and heat to boiling, stirring 1 minute. Add chicken and simmer over low heat.

Cook noodles in water according to package directions and drain. Top warm noodles with chicken and sauce.

Chicken Broccoli Casserole

Makes 6–8 servings

3 tablespoons butter or
   margarine
1 package chicken
   ramen noodles,
   crushed
1 (16-ounce) bag frozen
   chopped broccoli
4 chicken breasts,
   cooked and diced
1 box broccoli and
   cheese rice mix,
   cooked according to
   package directions
1 (4-ounce) can sliced
   mushrooms, drained
1 cup sour cream
1 cup grated cheddar
   cheese
1 (10.5-ounce) can
   cream of mushroom
   soup, condensed
$\frac{1}{2}$ cup milk
1 tablespoon
   Worcestershire sauce
Dash cayenne

Preheat oven to 350 degrees.

Prepare a 9 x 13-inch glass casserole dish with nonstick cooking spray.

In a medium frying pan, melt the butter over medium heat, add noodles, and stir to coat with butter. Cook, stirring until noodles are lightly browned. Set aside for topping.

In a large microwave-safe bowl, add the broccoli and fill with water until broccoli is completely covered. Microwave on high for 6 minutes; drain. Combine with remaining ingredients in a large bowl, mixing well and pour into the casserole dish. Sprinkle noodles on top of casserole and bake for 18–20 minutes, or until heated through and cheese is melted.

Chicken Diablo

Makes 2 servings

2 boneless, skinless chicken breasts, cut into chunks

1 package chicken ramen noodles, with seasoning packet

2 tablespoons butter or margarine

2 tablespoons flour

1 cup water mixed with seasoning packet

2 tablespoons chopped onion

1 tablespoon vinegar

1 tablespoon chopped parsley

¼ teaspoon tarragon leaves

¼ teaspoon thyme leaves

In a medium frying pan, brown chicken until done. Cook noodles in water according to package directions; drain and set aside.

In a small saucepan, heat butter over low heat until golden brown. Blend in flour, stirring until deep brown. Remove from heat. Add water mixture, onion, vinegar, and herbs, and heat to boiling, stirring 1 minute. Top warm noodles with chicken and sauce.

Chicken with Mushrooms

Makes 2–4 servings

¼ cup butter or margarine

1 pound boneless, skinless chicken tenders, cut into chunks

2 cups sliced fresh mushrooms

2 packages chicken ramen noodles, with seasoning packets

In a large frying pan, melt butter and brown chicken until done. Add mushrooms and sauté 5 minutes, or until tender.

Cook noodles in water according to package directions and drain. Add 1 seasoning packet. Top warm noodles with chicken and mushrooms.

Chicken Casserole

Makes 6–8 *servings*

3/4 cup water
1 (10.5-ounce) can
    cream of mushroom
    soup, condensed
1 (10.5-ounce) can
    cream of chicken
    soup, condensed
3 stalks celery, sliced
1 cup peas
1 carrot, sliced
3 packages chicken
    ramen noodles, with
    seasoning packets
1 pound chicken, cooked
    and chopped
1/2 cup Velveeta cheese,
    diced

In a large saucepan, heat water, soups, celery, peas, carrots, and 1 seasoning packet to boiling. Add noodles and simmer for 3 minutes. Add chicken and cheese, mix, and place in a 9 x 13-inch casserole dish. Heat in microwave on medium for 8–10 minutes.

Chicken Allemande

2 boneless, skinless chicken breasts, cut into chunks
2 packages chicken ramen noodles, with seasoning packets
2 tablespoons flour
Salt and pepper, to taste
1/8 teaspoon nutmeg
1 egg yolk
1 cup water mixed with 1 seasoning packet
2 tablespoons butter or margarine, melted
2 tablespoons cream
1 teaspoon lemon juice

In a frying pan, brown chicken until done.

Cook noodles in water according to package directions and drain.

In a medium saucepan, mix flour, salt, pepper, and nutmeg together. Beat egg yolk and water mixture together, and then stir into flour mixture. Heat to boiling and boil 1 minute, stirring constantly. Remove from heat. Stir in butter, cream, and lemon juice. Add chicken and simmer 2–3 minutes. Top warm noodles with chicken and sauce.

Herbed Chicken

Makes 4–5 *servings*

4 chicken breasts, cut
    into strips
1 tablespoon butter or
    margarine
1/2 cup diced carrots
1/4 cup diced onion
2 cups water
2 packages chicken
    ramen noodles,
    lightly crushed, with
    seasoning packets
Dash dried marjoram
Dash dried thyme
Pinch dried rosemary
Pinch rubbed sage

In a large frying pan, sauté the chicken in butter over medium heat until lightly brown. Add the carrots and onion; sauté until tender. Add water, 1 seasoning packet, and spices. Increase the heat and bring to a boil. Add noodles and continue to boil until water evaporates, stirring often.

Hot and Sour Ramen

Makes 1—2 servings

2½ cups water, divided
1 package oriental
  ramen noodles,
  lightly crushed,
  and with seasoning
  packet
½ teaspoon lemon juice
1 chicken breast,
  cooked and diced
¼ cup frozen peas
¼ cup frozen corn
1 teaspoon hot oil or
  Mongolian Fire Oil
1 tablespoon soy sauce
1 tablespoon cornstarch
2 eggs, beaten

In a large saucepan bring 2 cups of water to a boil. Add seasoning packet, lemon juice, chicken, peas, corn, hot oil, and soy sauce and cook for 3 minutes. Add noodles and continue to cook for 3 minutes more.

Mix cornstarch in remaining water. Slowly add to pan while stirring constantly. Let cook another minute or until mixture thickens. Slowly add the eggs, stirring constantly.

Cheesy Chicken Casserole

1/4 cup chopped onion
2 tablespoons butter or
   margarine
1 (10.75-ounce) can
   cream of chicken
   soup, condensed
1/2 cup milk
1 package chicken
   ramen noodles, with
   seasoning packet
1 cup grated sharp
   cheddar cheese
1 small can white
   chicken chunks,
   drained

Preheat oven to 350 degrees.

In a small saucepan, sauté onion in butter until tender. Add soup, milk, and just under 1/2 of the seasoning packet. Stir until smooth.

Cook noodles in water according to package directions and drain. Add cheese, chicken, and soup mixture. Stir until cheese is melted. Pour into a 1-quart greased casserole dish and bake 30 minutes.

Chicken 'n' Asparagus

Makes 4 servings

4 boneless, skinless chicken breasts
2 packages chicken ramen noodles, with seasoning packets
2 (10.75-ounce) cans cream of asparagus or mushroom soup, condensed
1 cup milk
½ pound fresh asparagus, cut up
1 cup grated cheddar cheese

In a large frying pan, brown chicken until done. Add remaining ingredients, except cheese and 1 seasoning packet. Simmer over low heat 10 minutes, or until noodles are done. Sprinkle with cheese before serving.

Garlic Chicken Toss

Makes 4–5 servings

5 green onions, chopped
2 tablespoons minced garlic
2 tablespoons butter or margarine
2 tablespoons olive oil
4 chicken breasts, diced
3 tablespoons lemon juice
3 tablespoons fresh parsley
2 packages chicken ramen noodles, with seasoning packets
4 cups water

In a large frying pan, sauté the onions and garlic in butter and oil until tender. Stir in the chicken, lemon juice, parsley, and 1 seasoning packet. Sauté until chicken is golden brown.

In a medium saucepan, bring water to a boil. Add noodles and cook for 3 minutes; drain. Add chicken mixture and toss.

Honey Grilled Chicken

Makes 3–6 *servings*

1 tablespoon creamy
   peanut butter
½ teaspoon red pepper
   flakes
¼ teaspoon ground
   ginger
1 teaspoon garlic
   powder
¼ cup honey
⅓ cup rice vinegar
2 tablespoons soy sauce
1 tablespoon sesame oil
2 tablespoons vegetable
   oil
3 boneless, skinless
   chicken breasts
3 cups water
2 medium carrots,
   sliced
2 cups broccoli florets
1 medium red bell
   pepper, sliced
1 package ramen
   noodles, any flavor
2 green onions, thinly
   sliced

Preheat the grill. In a medium bowl, combine peanut butter, red pepper flakes, ginger, garlic, honey, rice vinegar, soy sauce, and oils; stir to blend. Put 4 tablespoons of sauce in a ziplock bag for marinating; set aside remaining sauce. Place chicken in marinade in bag; seal and shake to coat. Refrigerate for at least 30 minutes or overnight.

In a large saucepan, bring water to a boil. Add carrots, broccoli, and bell pepper and cook over high heat until water comes to a rolling boil. Reduce heat to medium, add noodles and allow to cook for 3 minutes; drain. In a large bowl, combine the noodles and vegetables with the remaining sauce and onions. Toss to coat and cover with plastic wrap.

Grill chicken breasts over medium-hot coals for about 10 minutes, 5 minutes on each side or until done and juices run clear. Remove from grill and slice. Serve noodles topped with chicken slices.

Chicken Alfredo

Makes 2 servings

2 boneless, skinless chicken breasts, cut in strips

2 packages ramen noodles, any flavor

1 cup butter or margarine

1 cup cream

2 cups grated Parmesan cheese

2 tablespoons parsley flakes

½ teaspoon salt

Pepper

In a medium frying pan, brown chicken until done.

Cook noodles in water according to package directions and drain.

Heat butter and cream in a small saucepan over low heat until butter melts. Stir in remaining ingredients. Keep warm over low heat. Top warm noodles with chicken and sauce.

Creamy Chicken Noodles

Makes 2 servings

1 package chicken
    ramen noodles, with
    seasoning packet
1 (10.75-ounce) can
    cream of chicken
    soup, condensed
1/4 cup diced onion
1 small can chicken

Cook noodles in water according to package directions and drain.

In a small saucepan, heat soup, onion, chicken, and just under 1/2 of the seasoning packet, over medium heat 5 minutes. Top warm noodles with soup mixture.

Ramen Fajitas

Makes 2 servings

2 boneless, skinless
    chicken breasts, cut
    in strips
1 1/2 cups sliced onion
1 cup sliced red or
    green bell peppers
2 cups salsa
2 packages ramen
    noodles, any flavor
1/2 cup sour cream

In a large frying pan, brown chicken until done. Add onion, peppers, and salsa and cook over medium heat until vegetables are tender.

Cook noodles in water according to package directions and drain. Serve chicken mixture over warm noodles and top with sour cream.

Fiesta Chicken

Makes 2–4 servings

1 pound boneless, skinless chicken breasts, cut into chunks

Olive oil

½ cup corn

½ cup black beans, drained and rinsed

½ cup chopped red bell pepper

2 packages Cajun chicken ramen noodles, with seasoning packets

2–3 tablespoons sour cream

2 tablespoons salsa

In a large frying pan, brown chicken in olive oil. Add corn, black beans, and pepper. Sauté over low heat until heated through and vegetables are tender.

Cook noodles in water according to package directions and drain. Add seasoning packets. Combine noodles with chicken mixture. Stir in sour cream and salsa.

Chinese-Style Ramen

Makes 2 servings

½ **pound boneless,
skinless chicken
breasts, cut into
chunks**
¼ **cup water chestnut
halves**
½ **cup snow peas**
⅓ **cup bean sprouts**
¼ **cup celery**
2–3 **teaspoons oil**
1 **package oriental
ramen noodles, with
seasoning packet**
1 **tablespoon soy sauce**

In a medium frying pan, brown
chicken until done. Add water
chestnuts, snow peas, bean
sprouts, celery, and oil. Sauté until
vegetables are tender.

Cook noodles in water according
to package directions and drain.
Add seasoning packet. Spoon
vegetables over warm noodles and
sprinkle with soy sauce.

Thai Chicken

Makes 3–4 servings

4 cups water

2 packages chicken ramen noodles, with seasoning packets

$^1/_2$ cup shredded cooked chicken

1 carrot, thinly sliced with a vegetable peeler

$^1/_2$ cucumber, peeled, seeds removed, and thinly sliced

4 tablespoons spicy Thai peanut sauce

In a medium saucepan, bring water and 1 seasoning packet to a boil. Add noodles and cook for 3 minutes; drain. Toss noodles with remaining ingredients, adding more peanut sauce if needed until evenly coated, but not runny. Chill slightly or serve at room temperature.

Chicken Lo Mein

Makes 2 servings

1 tablespoon oil
1 tablespoon soy sauce
1 pound boneless, skin-less chicken breasts, cut into strips
½ cup sliced onion
½ cup chopped green bell pepper
¼ cup chopped carrot
1 package chicken ramen noodles, with seasoning packet

In a large frying pan, mix oil, soy sauce, and ½ of the seasoning packet. Add chicken and brown until done. Add vegetables to chicken, and cook until tender.

Cook noodles in water according to package directions and drain. Add noodles to chicken and vege-tables and cook over medium heat 3 minutes, stirring constantly.

Chicken Milano

Makes 2–4 servings

1 pound boneless, skinless chicken breasts, cut into chunks
2 teaspoons minced garlic
1 tablespoon olive oil
½ cup chopped sun-dried tomatoes
1 tablespoon basil
½ cup chicken broth
2 packages chicken ramen noodles, with seasoning packets
Salt and pepper, to taste

In a medium frying pan, brown chicken and garlic in oil until done. Add sun-dried tomatoes, basil, and chicken broth. Simmer over low heat 5 minutes.

Cook noodles in water according to package directions and drain. Add 1 seasoning packet. Serve chicken mixture over warm noodles. Season with salt and pepper.

Italian Chicken

Makes 2 servings

2 packages ramen noodles, any flavor
2 boneless, skinless chicken breasts, cut into chunks
1 cup Italian dressing, divided

Cook noodles in water according to package directions and drain. If possible, let chicken marinate overnight in $1/2$ cup dressing.

In a medium frying pan, cook chicken in the dressing until golden brown. Drizzle remaining dressing on noodles and toss. Top with chicken.

Caesar Chicken Ramen

Makes 2–4 servings

4 cups water
2 packages ramen noodles, any flavor
$1/2$ cup Caesar salad dressing
2 boneless, skinless chicken breasts, cooked and diced
$1/2$ cup croutons
$1/4$ cup cooked and crumbled bacon

In a medium saucepan, bring water to a boil. Add noodles and cook for 2 minutes; drain. Add dressing and toss to coat. Allow to chill in refrigerator for 1 hour. Add remaining ingredients and toss.

Turkey Pasta Pie

Makes 6 servings

½ pound ground turkey

¼ cup finely chopped onion

1 (14.5-ounce) can stewed tomatoes, with liquid

1 (8-ounce) can tomato sauce

½ teaspoon Italian seasoning

6 cups water

3 packages ramen noodles, any flavor

2 eggs, divided

1 tablespoon butter or margarine, melted

1 cup grated mozzarella cheese

1 cup creamy small-curd cottage cheese

1 (8-ounce) package frozen spinach, thawed and drained

¼ cup grated Parmesan cheese

Preheat oven to 350 degrees.

In a large frying pan, cook the turkey and onion over medium heat; drain. Stir in the tomatoes, tomato sauce, and Italian seasoning and bring to a boil; reduce heat. Cover and simmer for 10 minutes, stirring occasionally.

In a large saucepan, bring water to a boil. Add noodles and cook for 2 minutes; drain and set aside. Beat 1 egg and the butter in a large bowl. Add the noodles and mozzarella cheese; toss to mix. Place mixture into an ungreased 10-inch pie plate and press evenly on bottom and up side.

Mix the cottage cheese and remaining egg and then spread over the noodle mixture. Sprinkle with the spinach. Spoon turkey mixture evenly over top and then sprinkle with Parmesan cheese. Bake, uncovered, for 30 minutes, or until hot in center. Let stand 10 minutes before cutting.

Cheesy Turkey Casserole

Makes 1–2 servings

2 cups water
1 package oriental ramen noodles, with seasoning packet
¼ cup frozen mixed vegetables
¼ cup diced turkey
¼ cup Mexican cheese blend
4 slices Swiss cheese, diced
4 tablespoons Italian-style breadcrumbs

Preheat oven to 400 degrees.

Prepare an 8 x 8-inch casserole dish with nonstick cooking spray.

In a medium saucepan, bring water to a boil. Add the noodles and vegetables and cook for 3 minutes; drain. Add the seasoning packet, turkey, and Mexican cheese blend.

Pour half of the mixture into the casserole dish. Top with half the Swiss cheese. Add remaining mixture, top with remaining Swiss cheese and sprinkle with the breadcrumbs. Bake for 8–10 minutes or until crust has browned.

Turkey Gravy Noodles

Makes 1—2 servings

3 cups water, divided
**1 package beef ramen
    noodles, with
    seasoning packet**
**¼ cup sliced green
    onions**
**¼ cup diced green bell
    pepper**
¼ cup diced carrot
2 teaspoons olive oil
Dash pepper
1 cup turkey gravy
1 small tomato, diced

In a small saucepan, bring 2 cups water to a boil. Add noodles and cook for 2 minutes; drain and set aside.

Place the onions, bell pepper, and carrot in a sauté pan, add olive oil and toss to coat. Turn heat to medium and allow to cook for 1 minute, stirring regularly. Add the remaining water and pepper. Cook until there is only a little water left in the bottom of the pan, about 5 minutes. Stir in the seasoning packet. Add the turkey gravy and bring to a simmer. Serve noodles topped with the turkey gravy and tomatoes.

Leftover Thanksgiving Fried Ramen

Makes 1–2 servings

2 cups water
1 package chicken ramen noodles, with seasoning packet
4 tablespoons vegetable oil, divided
½ cup diced leftover turkey
½ cup leftover stuffing
½ cup chicken broth

In a small saucepan, bring water to a boil. Add noodles and cook for 3 minutes; drain and set aside.

In a large frying pan, add 2 tablespoons oil. Add the turkey and stuffing and cook over medium heat for 2–3 minutes, or until turkey begins to crisp on edges. Remove turkey and stuffing from pan and then add remaining oil. Place noodles in pan and toss to coat. Cook noodles for 1 minute and then stir in seasoning packet. Once the seasoning is mixed in evenly, add the turkey and stuffing. Gradually pour in the chicken broth; mix well. Cook another 30 seconds or until mixture is warmed through.

Turkey Ramen

Makes 2–4 *servings*

1 pound ground turkey
1 medium onion,
   chopped
2 tablespoons flour
2½ cups water
2 packages beef ramen
   noodles, lightly
   crushed, with
   seasoning packets
2 cups frozen vegetable
   stir-fry, thawed

In a large frying pan, cook turkey with the onion. Sprinkle flour over turkey and onion and blend thoroughly. Continue cooking meat mixture for 2–3 minutes. Add the water, noodles, seasoning packets, and vegetables. Cook for 5 minutes, or until noodles are tender. Let sit for 5 minutes or until gravy has thickened.

Pesto Turkey and Pasta

Makes 2–4 *servings*

4 cups water
2 packages ramen
noodles, any flavor
2 cups diced cooked
turkey breast
¹/₂ cup basil pesto
¹/₂ cup coarsely chopped
roasted red bell
peppers
Sliced black olives
(optional)

In a medium saucepan, bring water to a boil. Add noodles and cook for 3 minutes; drain. Add the turkey, pesto, and bell peppers to the noodles. Heat over low heat, stirring constantly, until hot. Serve with a garnish of olives, if desired.

Tomato-Basil
Turkey Casserole

Makes 6–8 *servings*

4 cups water

2 packages ramen noodles, any flavor

2 cups diced cooked turkey

1 (26-ounce) jar pasta sauce

1 medium zucchini, cut in half lengthwise, then cut into slices

1 (2.25-ounce) can sliced ripe olives, drained

1 teaspoon dried basil leaves

$\frac{1}{4}$ cup grated fresh Parmesan cheese

Preheat oven to 375 degrees.

Prepare a 2-quart casserole dish with nonstick cooking spray.

In a medium saucepan, bring water to a boil. Add noodles and cook for 3 minutes; drain. Add the turkey, pasta sauce, zucchini, olives, and basil; mix thoroughly. Add to casserole dish and cover. Bake for 30 minutes. Sprinkle with cheese. Bake, uncovered, for 15–20 minutes more, or until bubbly and thoroughly heated.

Fish & Seafood Dishes

Garlic Shrimp 'n' Veggies

Makes 2–4 servings

1 green bell pepper,
   thinly sliced
1 red bell pepper, thinly
   sliced
1/2 small onion, thinly
   sliced
1 1/2 tablespoons minced
   garlic
3–4 tablespoons olive
   oil
2 cups cooked small
   shrimp, peeled and
   deveined
2 packages oriental
   ramen noodles, with
   seasoning packets

In a large frying pan, sauté peppers,
onion, and garlic in olive oil until
tender. Add shrimp and 1 seasoning
packet. Simmer 3–5 minutes.

Cook noodles in water according
to package directions and drain.
Add 1/2 of remaining seasoning
packet. Serve shrimp mixture
over noodles.

Tuna Ramen Casserole

Makes 4–6 servings

- ½ cup butter or margarine, divided
- 1 cup onion, diced and divided
- 1½ cups stuffing mix
- 1 cup milk
- 1 cup chicken broth
- 1 tablespoon dry mustard
- 2 packages ramen noodles, any flavor, with seasoning packets
- 1 cup grated cheddar cheese
- 4 slices American cheese
- 2 (6-ounce) cans tuna, drained and flaked

Preheat oven to 375 degrees.

Add 6 tablespoons butter to a large frying pan. Over low heat, melt the butter and sauté ¾ cup onion. Cook for about 5 minutes, or until onion becomes translucent. Add stuffing to pan and toss to coat; set aside.

Combine the milk, broth, remaining butter, dry mustard, and seasoning packets in a medium saucepan and heat over low heat until hot, not boiling. Add the cheeses and remaining onion. Continue to cook on low heat until cheese melts. Break noodle packages in half and add to milk and broth mixture. Cook noodles until they separate easily. Add tuna and mix well. Pour tuna noodle mixture into a 9 x 13-inch casserole dish that has been prepared with nonstick cooking spray and sprinkle stuffing mixture over top. Bake for 30 minutes.

Salmon Ramen

Makes 2–4 servings

- **1 (14.5-ounce) can diced tomatoes, with liquid**
- **2 (5-ounce) cans salmon, drained**
- **2 tablespoons olive oil**
- **2 packages vegetable ramen noodles, with seasoning packets**
- **2 tablespoons oregano**
- **2 tablespoons minced garlic**
- **1 cup water**
- **2 tablespoons grated Parmesan cheese**

In a medium saucepan, combine the tomatoes, salmon, olive oil, seasoning packets, oregano, and garlic and bring to a simmer. Add the noodles and water. Cover and cook for 3 minutes. Serve sprinkled with Parmesan cheese.

Crab Lo Mein

Makes 4–6 *servings*

5¼ cups water, divided
2 packages chicken ramen noodles, with seasoning packets
1 medium onion, julienned
1 medium green bell pepper, julienned
2 cups frozen broccoli cuts, thawed
¼ cup sliced fresh mushrooms
2 tablespoons canola oil
1 tablespoon cornstarch
¼ cup soy sauce
1 (12-ounce) can crab meat, lightly chopped

In a medium saucepan, bring 4 cups water to a boil. Add noodles and cook for 3 minutes; drain and set aside.

In a large frying pan over medium heat, sauté the onion, bell pepper, broccoli, and mushrooms in oil for 3–4 minutes or until tender-crisp.

In a small bowl, combine the cornstarch, remaining water, seasoning packets, and soy sauce. Gradually add to pan and cook over medium heat until thick, stirring constantly. Add crab and continue to cook for 2 minutes more. Add to the noodles and then toss and serve.

Smoked Mussel Ramen

Makes 2–4 servings

4 cups water

2 packages chicken ramen noodles, with seasoning packets

3 tablespoons cooking oil

1 (6.5-ounce) can mushrooms, drained

1 (6.5-ounce) can smoked mussels, drained

1 tablespoon garlic powder

1 tablespoon onion powder

In a medium saucepan, bring water to a boil. Add noodles and cook for 3 minutes; drain, add the seasoning packets, stir, and set aside.

In a large frying pan or wok over medium heat, warm the oil. Add the mushrooms, mussels, garlic powder, and onion powder. Cook for 4 minutes, stirring often. Add noodles, lower heat slightly, stir, and then cook for 5 minutes more. Keep stirring until mushrooms and mussels are well blended with the noodles.

Swedish Ramen

Makes 3–4 *servings*

4 cups water
2 packages ramen noodles, any flavor
1 (7-ounce) can smoked Baltic herring in tomato sauce

In a small saucepan, bring water to a boil. Add noodles and cook for 3 minutes. Drain, add herring, and toss to coat.

Garlic Shrimp Ramen

Makes 1–2 *servings*

¼ pound pre-cooked shrimp
3 tablespoons butter or margarine
3 tablespoons minced garlic
1 package shrimp ramen noodles, with seasoning packet
2 cups water

In a medium frying pan, sauté shrimp in butter and garlic for 2–3 minutes, adding seasoning packet to taste.

In small saucepan, bring water to a boil. Add noodles and cook for 3 minutes; drain and add to shrimp mixture. Toss and serve.

Cajun Seafood Noodles

Makes 4-6 *servings*

2 cups water
Pinch sugar
1 teaspoon butter or
    margarine
1/4 teaspoon celery salt
1 teaspoon minced
    garlic
2 packages shrimp
    ramen noodles, with
    seasoning packets
1 (6-ounce) can shrimp,
    drained
1 chicken breast,
    cooked and cubed
1/4 cup cooked and cubed
    Cajun sausage

In a medium saucepan, bring the
water, sugar, butter, celery salt, garlic, and seasoning packets to a boil.
Add the noodles, shrimp, chicken,
and sausage. Cook for 3 minutes.

Teriyaki Tuna Ramen

Makes 2–4 servings

2 cups water
1 package ramen
    noodles, any flavor
1 (6-ounce) can tuna,
    drained
1 carrot, thinly sliced
1/4 teaspoon freshly
    chopped ginger
1/4 teaspoon honey
1 tablespoon teriyaki
    sauce
1 green onion, thinly
    sliced

In a small saucepan, bring water to a boil. Add noodles and cook for 3 minutes; drain, add tuna, and set aside.

In a small saucepan, steam the carrot with the ginger and honey in enough water to barely cover carrots. Cook until tender-crisp, or about 2–3 minutes. Drain and add to tuna and noodles. Top with teriyaki sauce and toss. Serve garnished with onion.

Ramen Clam Chowder Pie

Makes 6–8 servings

2 cups water
1 package ramen
    noodles, any flavor
1 (10.75-ounce) can New
    England–style clam
    chowder
1 (9-inch) pre-cooked
    piecrust
1/4 cup grated cheddar
    cheese
10 Ritz crackers,
    crushed

Preheat oven to 350 degrees.

In a small saucepan, bring water to a boil. Add noodles and cook for 3 minutes; drain. Add clam chowder and toss. Pour into pie crust and top with cheese and crackers. Bake for 15 minutes, or until crackers are visibly toasted.

Coconut Curry Shrimp

Makes 2–4 servings

- **4 cups water**
- **2 packages ramen noodles, any flavor**
- **$1/2$ cup coconut milk**
- **$1/3$ cup creamy peanut butter**
- **$1^1/2$ teaspoon curry**
- **1 lime, juiced**
- **1 pound large shrimp, cooked and cleaned**
- **$1/2$ seedless cucumber, julienned**
- **4 scallions, sliced**

Bring water to a boil in a large frying pan. Add noodles and cover. Remove from heat and let stand 5 minutes.

Whisk the coconut milk, peanut butter, curry, and lime juice in a medium bowl to blend. Drain noodles and add shrimp, cucumber, scallions, and coconut milk mixture; toss to coat. Serve at room temperature.

Creamy Mushroom Shrimp Ramen

Makes 2 servings

**1 package oriental
    ramen noodles, with
    seasoning packet**
**1 (10.75-ounce) can
    cream of mushroom
    soup, condensed**
**1 (6-ounce) can shrimp,
    drained**
**1 cup sliced fresh
    mushrooms**

Cook noodles in water according
to package directions; do not drain.
Add soup, shrimp, mushrooms, and
½ of the seasoning packet. Cook 10
minutes over medium heat.

Shrimp Ramen

Makes 2 servings

1 package oriental
    ramen noodles, with
    seasoning packet
1 (10.75-ounce) can
    cream of celery soup,
    condensed
1 (6-ounce) can shrimp,
    drained
Salt and pepper, to taste

Cook noodles in water according to package directions and drain. Add just under $\frac{1}{2}$ of the seasoning packet. Add soup, shrimp, salt, and pepper. Cook 10 minutes over medium heat.

Spinach Crab Ramen

Makes 2–4 servings

2 cups water
2 packages vegetable
    ramen noodles, with
    seasoning packets
1 (12-ounce) package
    imitation crabmeat
1 (14-ounce) can
    spinach, drained

In a medium saucepan, bring water to a boil. Add noodles with seasoning packets, crab, and spinach. Cook for 3 minutes.

Cheesy Salmon Noodles

Makes 2 servings

**1 package ramen
noodles, any flavor**
**1 (10.75-ounce) can
cream of mushroom
soup, condensed**
¹/₂ cup milk
**1 small can salmon,
drained**
**1 cup cooked spinach or
asparagus**
**1 cup grated cheddar
cheese**

Cook noodles in water according
to package directions and drain.
Add soup, milk, salmon, and broccoli. Simmer 5 minutes. Sprinkle
cheese over top and serve.

Cheesy Tuna Ramen

Makes 2–4 servings

**2 packages ramen
noodles, any flavor**

**2 (10.75-ounce) cans
cream of mushroom
soup, condensed**

1 cup milk

**2 (6-ounce) cans tuna,
drained**

2 cups peas

**2 cups grated cheddar
cheese**

Cook noodles in water according
to package directions and drain.
Add soup, milk, tuna, and peas.
Simmer 5 minutes. Sprinkle cheese
over top and serve.

Tuna Noodle Casserole

Makes 2–4 servings

2 (6-ounce) cans tuna,
  drained
1 cup grated cheddar
  cheese
1/2 cup water
1 cup milk
2 eggs, beaten
2 packages chicken
  ramen noodles,
  broken up, with
  seasoning packets
10–20 saltine crackers,
  crushed

Preheat oven to 350 degrees.

In a medium bowl, mix tuna, cheese, water, milk, eggs, and 1 seasoning packet. Transfer mixture to a casserole dish. Add broken uncooked noodles. Bake 15 minutes, stirring occasionally. Sprinkle crackers over top and bake 5 minutes more.

Twice-Baked Tuna Casserole

Makes 2—4 servings

2 packages ramen noodles, any flavor, with seasoning packets

2 (6-ounce) cans tuna, drained

1 cup grated cheddar cheese

1/2 cup chopped onion

1 cup crushed potato chips

Preheat oven to 350 degrees.

Cook noodles in water according to package directions and drain. Season with 1 seasoning packet. Mix tuna, cheese, onion, and noodles together in a small casserole dish and bake 15–20 minutes. Sprinkle chips over top and bake 15 minutes more.

Vegetables
& Sides

Cheesy Vegetable Ramen

Makes 2 servings

1 package ramen noodles, any flavor, with seasoning packet

1 cup frozen mixed vegetables

1 tablespoon water

1 small jar creamy cheese sauce, condensed

Cook noodles in water according to package directions and drain. Add ½ of the seasoning packet and set aside.

In a medium frying pan, cook vegetables in water until tender. Add cheese sauce to vegetables and heat through. Stir in noodles.

Bok Choy Ramen

Makes 1–2 servings

- ¼ cup vegetable oil
- 1 package ramen noodles, any flavor, crushed
- ⅓ cup olive oil
- ½ cup sugar
- 1 teaspoon soy sauce
- ¼ cup vinegar
- 1 head bok choy, thinly sliced
- ¼ cup sliced green onion
- ½ cup sliced almonds

Heat oil in a large frying pan. Add noodles and fry until lightly brown, stirring constantly.

In a small saucepan, combine olive oil, sugar, soy sauce, and vinegar to make dressing. Cook over low heat for 2 minutes. Place bok choy and noodles in a bowl and drizzle with dressing. Toss to coat and serve.

Spinach Parmesan Ramen

Makes 3–4 servings

4½ cups water, divided
2 packages vegetable
   ramen noodles, with
   seasoning packets
¼ cup chopped onion
1 teaspoon minced
   garlic
¼ cup frozen spinach,
   thawed and drained
4 tablespoons milk
1 tablespoon cream
   cheese
¼ cup grated Parmesan
   cheese
¼ cup grated mozzarella
   cheese

In a large saucepan, bring 4 cups water to a boil. Add noodles and cook 3 minutes; drain and set aside.

In a large saucepan, add remaining water and 1 seasoning packet, stirring until dissolved. Bring to a boil over medium heat. Add onion and garlic and let simmer for 5 minutes. Stir in spinach and cook for 2 minutes more. Add milk and cheeses, stirring until cheese is melted. Add noodles and toss until coated.

Veggie Sauté

Makes 2 servings

**1 package ramen
noodles, any flavor,
with seasoning
packet**
1/2 cup sliced onion
1/2 cup diced tomato
**1 (4-ounce) can
mushrooms, drained**
**1/2 cup chopped green
bell pepper**
**1 teaspoon garlic
powder**
2 tablespoons oil

Cook noodles in water according
to package directions and drain.
Season noodles with 1/2 of the seasoning packet.

In a frying pan, sauté vegetables in
garlic powder and oil over low heat
until tender. Stir in warm noodles
and serve.

Asian Noodle Toss

Makes 1—2 servings

2 cups water
1 package vegetable
    ramen noodles
4 baby carrots,
    julienned
$^{1}/_{2}$ cup sugar snap peas
1 (4-ounce) can
    mandarin oranges
1 tablespoon soy sauce
1 tablespoon orange
    jelly
1 tablespoon cider
    vinegar

In a small saucepan, bring water to a boil. Add noodles, carrots, and peas and cook for 3 minutes: drain and place in a bowl. Add the oranges, reserving the juice in a small bowl. To the juice, add the soy sauce, jelly, and vinegar; mix thoroughly. Drizzle over noodles, toss and serve warm.

Broccoli and Ramen Noodles

Makes 2–4 *servings*

- 2 cups water
- 1 package vegetable ramen noodles, with seasoning packet
- 1 tablespoon corn oil
- 4 cups broccoli
- 1/4 cup lemon juice
- 1/4 cup honey
- 1/2 teaspoon pepper
- 1 cup unsalted peanuts, chopped

In a small saucepan, bring water to a boil. Add noodles and cook 3 minutes; drain and toss in oil. Place broccoli in a microwave-safe bowl and add enough water to cover. Microwave on high for 4 minutes; drain well and add noodles.

In a small bowl, combine the lemon juice, honey, pepper, and seasoning packet; mix thoroughly. Drizzle over broccoli and noodles. Top with peanuts and toss to coat. Serve warm.

Yakisoba

Makes 4–6 servings

6 cups water
4 packages ramen noodles, any flavor
$1/2$ teaspoon sesame oil
1 tablespoon canola oil
2 tablespoons chile paste
2 cloves garlic, chopped
$1/2$ cup soy sauce, divided
1 onion, sliced lengthwise into eighths
$1/2$ medium head cabbage, coarsely chopped
2 carrots, coarsely chopped

In a large saucepan, bring water to a boil. Add noodles and cook 3 minutes; drain and set aside.

In a large frying pan, combine the oils and chile paste and then stir-fry for 30 seconds. Add the garlic and $1/4$ cup soy sauce and stir-fry 30 seconds more. Add the onion, cabbage, and carrots. Stir-fry until cabbage begins to wilt. Stir in remaining soy sauce and cooked noodles. Continue to cook until noodles barely begin to crisp.

Olive and Red Pepper Ramen

Makes 4–6 servings

4 cups water
2 packages ramen noodles, any flavor
1 medium red bell pepper, chopped
3/4 cup sliced fresh mushrooms
1/2 cup chopped onion
1 1/2 teaspoons minced garlic
1 tablespoon vegetable oil
15 stuffed green olives, sliced

In a medium saucepan, bring water to a boil. Add noodles and cook for 3 minutes; drain and set aside.

In a large frying pan, sauté the bell pepper, mushrooms, onion, and garlic in oil, until softened. Add olives and noodles; toss and serve.

Spicy Lime Ramen

Makes 1–2 servings

2 cups water
1 package chili ramen
   noodles, with
   seasoning packet
Pinch garlic powder
Pinch cayenne pepper
1 green onion, sliced
1/2 teaspoon finely
   chopped cilantro
1/2 lime, juiced

In a small saucepan, bring water to a boil. Add noodles and cook for 3 minutes; drain and reserve 1/4 cup of the water.

In a small bowl, mix seasoning packet, garlic, and cayenne; add to reserved water and mix until seasonings have dissolved. Add to noodles and toss to coat. Top with onion, cilantro, and lime juice, to taste.

Garlic Cilantro Noodles

Makes 2–4 servings

2 packages oriental ramen noodles, with seasoning packets
2 cups fresh or frozen mixed vegetables
1 teaspoon minced garlic
2 tablespoons fresh chopped cilantro

In a large saucepan, cook noodles and vegetables in water together according to package directions and drain. Add garlic, cilantro, and seasoning packets. Simmer over low heat 5 minutes, stirring occasionally.

Corny Cheese Noodles

Makes 2 servings

1 package ramen noodles, any flavor, with seasoning packet
1½ cups grated cheddar cheese
1 (14-ounce) can creamed corn

Cook noodles in water according to package directions and drain. Add seasoning packet.

In a medium saucepan, heat cheese and corn over medium heat. Mix with warm noodles.

Pad Thai

Makes 2—4 *servings*

2 packages vegetable ramen noodles, with seasoning packets
3 tablespoons soy sauce
2 tablespoons sesame oil
1 (16-ounce) package extra firm tofu, cubed
4 cups water
1 (32-ounce) bag frozen stir-fry vegetables
Peanut sauce

In a small bowl, combine 1 seasoning packet, soy sauce, and sesame oil. Transfer to a ziplock bag and add tofu. Seal and toss to coat. Allow to marinate for 1–2 hours.

In a medium saucepan, bring water to a boil. Add noodles and cook 3 minutes; drain and set aside.

Remove tofu from marinade and pour remaining marinade into a large frying pan or wok. Add vegetables and cook over medium heat until vegetables become soft. Add tofu and continue to cook, stirring gently, until tofu is heated. Add noodles and allow them to cook until they absorb most of the remaining liquid in the pan. Transfer to a bowl and toss with peanut sauce.

Italian Ramen Patties

Makes 4 servings

8 cups water
4 packages ramen noodles, any flavor
2 teaspoons olive oil, divided
4 medium carrots, cut into thin strips
1 teaspoon dried basil leaves
¼ teaspoon salt
1 (10-ounce) package frozen chopped spinach, thawed and drained
2 eggs, slightly beaten
½ cup ricotta cheese
¼ cup grated Parmesan cheese
¼ teaspoon pepper
2 cups spaghetti sauce, warmed

In a large saucepan, bring water to a boil. Add noodles and cook for 2 minutes; drain and set aside.

Heat 1 teaspoon oil in a large frying pan over medium heat. Cook carrots, basil, salt, and spinach for 2 minutes, stirring occasionally, until carrots are tender-crisp.

In a large bowl, mix the noodles, eggs, cheeses, and pepper. Shape pasta mixture into 4 patties, each about 1-inch thick.

Heat remaining oil in a large frying pan over medium-high heat. Cook patties for 6–8 minutes, turning after 4 minutes, until golden brown. Top patties with vegetable mixture and spaghetti sauce.

Mushroom and Zucchini Ramen

Makes 6 servings

6 cups water

3 packages vegetable ramen noodles, with seasoning packets

2 medium zucchini, thinly sliced

1/2 pound fresh mushrooms, sliced

2 green onions, chopped

1 tablespoon minced garlic

2 tablespoons butter or margarine

1 tablespoon olive oil

1 large tomato, diced

2 teaspoons minced fresh basil

1 cup grated provolone cheese

3 tablespoons grated Parmesan cheese

In a medium saucepan, bring water to a boil. Add noodles and cook for 3 minutes; drain and set aside.

In a large frying pan over medium heat, sauté the zucchini, mushrooms, onions, and garlic in butter and oil for 4 minutes. Add the tomato, basil, and 2 seasoning packets and stir. Cover and simmer for 3 minutes. Add the noodles and cheese. Toss to coat and serve.

Broccoli-Cauliflower Ramen

Makes 2 servings

1 (10.75-ounce) can cream of celery soup, condensed
¹/₂ cup milk
1 cup broccoli pieces
¹/₂ cup cauliflower pieces
¹/₂ cup sliced carrots
1 package ramen noodles, any flavor, with seasoning packet

In a large saucepan, heat soup and milk to boiling. Stir in vegetables and heat to boiling. Reduce heat and simmer 15 minutes.

Cook noodles in water according to package directions and drain. Add seasoning packet. Top warm noodles with soup mixture.

Ohm Raisu Ramen

Makes 1–2 servings

2 cups water
1 package vegetable ramen noodles, with seasoning packet
3 eggs
2 cups cooked rice
¼ cup bean sprouts
1 (5-ounce) can sliced water chestnuts, drained

In a small saucepan, bring water to a boil. Add noodles with seasoning packet and cook 2 minutes.

Fry the eggs, breaking the yolks and cooking until eggs have completely cooked; set aside. Put rice into bottom of a large microwave-safe bowl and then add noodles with broth. Slice the eggs into thin strips and add to noodles. Add the bean sprouts and water chestnuts. Place in microwave and cook on high for 1 minute.

Hollandaise Vegetables

Makes 2 servings

**1 package chicken
ramen noodles, with
seasoning packet**

2 egg yolks

**3 tablespoons lemon
juice**

**$1/2$ cup butter or
margarine, divided**

**1 cup fresh or frozen
mixed vegetables**

Cook noodles in water according to package directions, and drain.

In a small saucepan, whisk egg yolks and lemon juice briskly with a fork. Add $1/2$ of the butter and stir over low heat until melted. Add remaining butter, stirring briskly until melted and sauce thickens.

Cook vegetables and drain. Top warm noodles with vegetables and sauce.

Pan Fried Noodles

Makes 2–4 servings

2 packages oriental ramen noodles, with seasoning packets
1 cup frozen peas and carrots
2 eggs
1–2 teaspoons oil
2–3 tablespoons soy sauce

Cook noodles in water according to package directions and drain. Add seasoning packets. Heat vegetables in microwave until heated through and add to warm noodles.

In a small frying pan, fry eggs in oil; break yolk and cook until hard, flipping occasionally. Cut eggs into pieces. Stir into noodle mixture. Sprinkle soy sauce over top and stir together, adding more if necessary.

Tomato Sauté

Makes 2–4 servings

**2 packages ramen
noodles, any flavor,
with seasoning
packets**
**1 cup butter or
margarine**
**2 (14.5-ounce) cans
diced tomatoes**
**2 teaspoons minced
garlic**

Cook noodles in water according
to package directions and drain.

In a large frying pan, melt butter.
Add tomatoes, garlic, seasoning
packets, and noodles and stir. Season with salt and pepper. Simmer
5 minutes.

Chinese Veggie Noodles

Makes 2 servings

1 package oriental ramen noodles, with seasoning packet
1 cup frozen stir-fry vegetables
1½ teaspoons olive oil
1 tablespoon soy sauce

In a small saucepan, cook noodles in water according to package directions and drain. Add seasoning packet.

In a small frying pan, sauté vegetables in olive oil until heated through and add to warm noodles. Sprinkle soy sauce over top and stir together. Season with salt and pepper.

Chinese Fried Noodles

Makes 1–2 servings

2 cups water
1 package oriental ramen noodles, with seasoning packet
2 tablespoons oil
1 heaping teaspoon minced garlic
1 tablespoon soy sauce
1 teaspoon oyster sauce

In small saucepan, bring water to a boil. Add noodles and cook for 3 minutes, drain and set aside.

In a medium frying pan or wok, heat oil over medium heat. Add garlic, half the seasoning packet, soy sauce, and oyster sauce. Add noodles and fry until noodles begin to crisp, about 3–4 minutes.

Quick and Easy Breakfast Ramen

Makes 1–2 servings

Water
1 package vegetable ramen noodles, with seasoning packet
4 tomato slices
1 green onion, sliced
2 eggs, beaten

Put just enough water in a small saucepan to cover the brick of ramen noodles. When the water comes to a boil, stir in seasoning packet and add the brick of noodles. Cover with tomatoes, sprinkle with onion, and pour eggs on the top. Put on a lid and wait for it to boil just enough for the egg to cook to your liking.

Spinach and Egg Ramen

Makes 1–2 servings

2 cups water
**1 package chicken
    ramen noodles, with
    seasoning packet**
**¼ cup frozen spinach,
    thawed and drained**
Dash soy sauce
Dash rice vinegar
1 egg

In a small saucepan, bring water to a boil, add noodles, and cook for 3 minutes or until done. Drain and set aside.

In a medium frying pan over medium heat, combine the spinach, soy sauce, vinegar, and about ¼–⅓ of the seasoning packet; toss.

Beat egg in a bowl and then add to the pan; continue cooking until egg begins to set. Add noodles and cook until noodles begin to brown, stirring regularly.

Fried Ramen and Eggs

Makes 1–2 servings

2 cups water
1 package ramen
    noodles, any flavor,
    with seasoning
    packet
2 dashes sesame oil
1/4 cup cooking oil
1 tablespoon finely
    chopped onion
1 tablespoon finely
    chopped green bell
    pepper
1 tablespoon finely
    chopped red bell
    pepper
2 eggs
1 tablespoon soy sauce

In a small saucepan, bring water to a boil and cook noodles, until tender but still firm; drain. Toss noodles with sesame oil and half of seasoning packet (save rest of packet for something else); set noodles aside.

Heat just enough cooking oil to cover bottom of frying pan over medium-low heat until hot. Add noodles, spreading out carefully. Cook until they begin to crisp on the bottom, turn over carefully with spatula and separate them slightly, adding a bit more oil if they start to stick. Sprinkle onion and bell peppers over the noodles. Beat eggs with soy sauce.

Pour eggs over noodles and cook, mixing gently with a fork or spatula, until done to your liking.

Ricotta Frittata

6 cups water
2 cups frozen green peas
3 packages mushroom ramen noodles, with seasoning packets
1 (15-ounce) container part-skim ricotta cheese
3 eggs
½ cup milk
½ cup grated Parmesan cheese
¼ teaspoon pepper
1 (14.5-ounce) can Italian-style diced tomatoes

Preheat oven to 400 degrees.

Lightly prepare a 13 x 9-inch baking dish with nonstick cooking spray. In a large saucepan, bring water to a boil. Add peas and return to a boil. Break up noodles as directed on package and add to pan. Cook 3 minutes, stirring occasionally, or until noodles and peas are tender; drain.

Mix ricotta, eggs, milk, cheese, pepper, and 2 seasoning packets in a large bowl until blended. Stir in noodles and peas. Transfer mixture to baking dish and spread evenly. Bake about 20 minutes or until set. Heat tomatoes in the microwave for 1 minute or until hot. Spoon over frittata. Cut in squares to serve.

Grilled Ramen

Makes 2—4 servings

1 package ramen
   noodles, chicken,
   pork, or beef with
   seasoning packet
2 tablespoons soy sauce
Dash hot sauce
Dash sesame oil
1 tablespoon marmalade
¼ cup hot water, not
   boiling

In a ziplock bag, combine the seasoning packet, soy sauce, hot sauce, sesame oil, marmalade, and hot water. Mix thoroughly. Add brick of noodles and seal completely. Tilt bag to allow marinade to coat the entire brick. Allow to sit for at least 15 minutes but no longer than 30 minutes. Flip occasionally to prevent marinade from pooling in one spot.

Over a medium flame, grill noodle brick for 3 minutes each side or until char marks appear. Be sure the brick is not stuck to the grill or it may pull apart when you try to flip or remove it. Serve with remaining marinade as "au jus" or place in a bowl and add 1 cup of boiling water for a less crunchy dish.

Stuffed Tomatoes

8 large tomatoes
Dash salt
1 cup water
1 package chicken or
vegetable ramen
noodles, crushed
and with seasoning
packet
1/2 pound sliced fresh
mushrooms
2 tablespoons butter or
margarine
1 tablespoon flour
1/2 cup half-and-half
2 tablespoons
breadcrumbs
1 cup grated cheddar
cheese, divided

Preheat oven to 400 degrees.

Cut tomatoes in half, scoop out pulp, and set aside. Sprinkle tomatoes with salt and invert on paper towels and let drain, about 15 minutes.

In a small saucepan, bring water to boil, add noodles, and let cook for 2 minutes; drain and set aside.

In a medium frying pan, sauté mushrooms in butter for 5 minutes. Add seasoning packet and flour; gradually stir in the half-and-half. Bring to a simmer stirring constantly until thick, about 2 minutes. Remove from heat and stir in breadcrumbs and 1/2 cup cheese. Add noodles and mix. Spoon into tomato cups and sprinkle with remaining cheese. Prepare two 9 x 13-inch baking dishes with nonstick cooking spray. Place tomatoes in dishes and bake, uncovered, for 10 minutes.

Tuna Noodle Spread

Makes 6–8 servings

1 cup water

1 package beef ramen
  noodles, crushed
  and with seasoning
  packet

2 hard-boiled eggs,
  chopped

1 (6-ounce) can tuna,
  drained

3 tablespoons
  mayonnaise

24 saltine crackers

In a small saucepan, bring water to a boil. Add noodles and let boil for 2 minutes; drain.

In a medium bowl, combine the seasoning packet, eggs, tuna, and mayonnaise. Add the noodles and thoroughly mix together. If it seems dry, add more mayonnaise. The mixture should be just moist enough to hold together. Serve on saltine crackers.

Baked Ramen Cakes

Makes 8–10 *cakes*

½ cup water
1 package ramen noodles, any flavor, with seasoning packet
¼ cup olive oil

Preheat oven to 250 degrees.

In a small saucepan, bring water to a low simmer over medium heat. Reduce heat to medium low and add noodles. Cook for 30 seconds, flip and sprinkle with half the seasoning packet. Continue to cook until water is nearly gone. Sprinkle with remaining seasoning. Add olive oil and gently turn noodles in pan until noodles are well covered in oil; drain oil. Use a spoon to remove noodles from pan and place on a baking sheet. Arrange so noodles are in small circular shapes. Bake in oven for 30 minutes or until light brown and crispy. Use on salads, soups, or stir-fry.

Sweet and Salty Ramen

Makes 4–6 servings

4 cups water
2 packages oriental ramen noodles, with seasoning packets
1¹/₂ tablespoons soy sauce
2 teaspoons brown sugar
1 tablespoon cold butter or margarine

In a large saucepan, bring water to a boil. Add noodles and let boil for 2 minutes; drain and set aside.

In the same pan add the soy sauce, brown sugar, seasoning packets, and a touch of water. Remove from heat and add cold butter. Stir until melted. Add noodles and toss. Serve with chicken or steak.

Twisted Ramen

Makes 10–15 *twists*

4 cups water, divided
2 packages ramen
   noodles, any flavor,
   with seasoning
   packets
3 eggs, divided
1½ cups flour
1 teaspoon salt
4 cups vegetable oil

In a medium saucepan, bring 3 cups water to a boil. Add noodles and let cook for 2 minutes; drain and set aside.

In a medium bowl, make a batter using 1 egg, flour, 1 seasoning packet, and remaining water. Beat remaining eggs in a large bowl. Add noodles, and toss to coat.

In a large frying pan, heat the oil. Separate and twist or braid 4–5 noodles together, dry slightly on paper towels, and then dip noodle twists in batter. Fry till golden brown. Serve with butter or your favorite dip.

Ramen Pancakes

Makes 8 servings

2 cups water
1 package ramen
   noodles, any flavor,
   with seasoning
   packet
1 medium zucchini,
   shredded
2 scallions, cut in long
   narrow strips
1 medium carrot,
   shredded
2 eggs, beaten
2 tablespoons flour
2 tablespoons vegetable
   oil, divided

In a small saucepan, bring water to a boil. Add noodles and let boil for 2 minutes; drain and place in a medium bowl. Stir in the zucchini, scallions, carrot, eggs, flour, and half of the seasoning packet.

Heat 1 tablespoon oil in a large nonstick frying pan over medium-high heat. Using half of the noodle mixture, make 4 pancakes. Fry 2–3 minutes per side. Repeat, using remaining oil. Serve as a side with entrees based on ramen flavor.

Family
Favorites

Breakfast Casserole

9 eggs, separated
1 teaspoon plus
2 tablespoons
vegetable oil, divided
1 teaspoon sugar
3 cups water
2 packages mushroom
or chicken ramen
noodles, with
seasoning packets
1 teaspoon soy sauce
3 green onions, sliced
and divided
1 (8-ounce) package
sliced fresh
mushrooms
1 teaspoon ginger
1 teaspoon garlic
powder

Preheat oven to 350 degrees.

Prepare an 8 x 8-inch glass baking dish with nonstick cooking spray. In a small mixing bowl, whisk 3 egg yolks with 9 egg whites. Beat in 1 teaspoon oil and sugar to egg mixture; set aside.

In large saucepan, boil water. Add noodles and cook 3 minutes.

Heat a medium frying pan over medium heat with 2 tablespoons oil and soy sauce. Setting ⅓ of the onions to the side for topping later, sauté the mushrooms and onions in the pan. Stir in ginger and garlic. Sauté until mushrooms begin to darken a little; remove from heat.

Drain the cooked noodles and then stir in one of the seasoning packets. Add the contents of the frying pan to the saucepan of noodles and mix well. Slowly add the egg mixture into the saucepan, stirring well. Replace saucepan over medium heat for a couple of minutes, until the liquid egg around the mixture begins to form tiny bubbles. Immediately transfer the mixture to the baking dish. Top with the reserved onions. Bake approximately 15 minutes, or until top begins to brown and eggs are cooked. Remove from oven and allow to cool completely before serving.

Meaty Spaghetti

Makes 2–4 *servings*

2 packages ramen noodles, any flavor
1–2 cups spaghetti sauce
1 pound ground beef or sausage, browned and drained
Grated Parmesan cheese

Cook noodles in water according to package directions and drain.

In a medium saucepan, heat sauce and cooked beef over medium heat 3–5 minutes, or until heated through. Spoon sauce over warm noodles and then sprinkle with cheese.

Garlic Noodle Sauté

Makes 2–4 servings

2 packages chicken ramen noodles, with seasoning packets
2 cups sliced fresh mushrooms
½ red onion, sliced
1 tablespoon minced garlic
Olive oil

Cook noodles in water according to package directions and drain. Season with 1 seasoning packet.

In a large frying pan, sauté mushrooms, onion, and garlic in olive oil until tender. Add warm noodles and sauté 2 minutes.

Creamy Alfredo Noodles

Makes 2–3 servings

2 packages ramen noodles, any flavor
1 cup butter or margarine
1 cup cream
2 cups freshly grated Parmesan cheese
1 teaspoon garlic salt
Italian seasoning, to taste
Pepper, to taste

Cook noodles in water according to package directions and drain.

In a medium saucepan, heat butter and cream over low heat until butter is melted. Stir in remaining ingredients. Simmer sauce 5 minutes. Serve sauce over warm noodles.

Mexican Casserole

Makes 2–4 servings

2 packages chicken
    mushroom ramen
    noodles, with
    seasoning packets
1 cup cubed Monterey
    Jack cheese
$1/2$ cup diced green
    chiles
$1/4$ cup sliced black
    olives
1 cup sour cream
1 cup grated cheddar
    cheese
$1/4$ cup grated Parmesan
    cheese
$1/2$ cup crushed corn
    chips

Preheat oven to 400 degrees.

Cook noodles in water according to package directions; rinse with cold water. Combine noodles, seasoning packets, Monterey Jack cheese, chiles, and olives. Stir in sour cream. Spoon noodle mixture into a greased casserole dish. Sprinkle with remaining cheeses and chips. Bake 20 minutes, or until brown and bubbly.

Cheesy Omelet

Makes 1–2 servings

2 cups water
1 package vegetable ramen noodles, with seasoning packet
1 tablespoon butter or margarine
2 eggs
1/8 cup milk
2 slices Velveeta cheese

In a small saucepan, bring water to a boil. Add noodles and cook for 2 minutes; drain.

Put butter in a medium microwave-safe bowl, microwave for 20–30 seconds, or until melted. Add eggs, milk, and 1/4 of the seasoning packet; whisk to combine. Add noodles and toss.

Pour contents into a frying pan heated to medium-high and cover. Flip omelets when underside begins to separate from pan and becomes brown. Top with cheese and return cover. Once bottom begins to brown, fold over and serve.

Pizza Pasta

Makes 2–4 servings

**2 packages ramen
   noodles, any flavor**
**2–3 cups spaghetti
   sauce**
**20–25 pepperoni slices,
   halved**
**3/4 cup chopped green
   bell pepper**
**1/2 cup grated cheddar
   cheese**
**1 cup grated mozzarella
   cheese**

Preheat oven to 350 degrees.

Cook noodles in water according to package directions and drain.

In a large saucepan, combine sauce, pepperoni, pepper, and cheddar cheese. Stir constantly until cheese is melted. Place noodles in a lightly greased 8 x 8-inch pan. Pour sauce mixture over top. Sprinkle with mozzarella cheese. Bake 15 minutes, or until cheese is melted.

Cheesy Noodles

Makes 2–4 servings

**2 packages ramen
noodles, any flavor**
**1 cup cubed American
processed cheese**
1/2–3/4 cup milk
Salt and pepper, to taste

Cook noodles in water according to package directions and drain. Add cheese and milk and stir until cheese is melted. Season with salt and pepper.

Lasagna

Makes 2–4 servings

**2 packages ramen
noodles, any flavor**
2 cups spaghetti sauce
1 cup ricotta cheese
**1 cup grated mozzarella
cheese**
1 cup Parmesan cheese

Preheat oven to 350 degrees.

Cook noodles in water according to package directions and drain. Stir sauce into noodles.

In an 8 x 8-inch pan, layer half of the noodle mixture, ricotta, mozzarella, and Parmesan cheeses. Repeat layers. Bake 20 minutes.

Primavera Pasta

Makes 2–4 servings

1/4 cup slivered almonds
1 cup chopped broccoli
1 cup snow peas
1 cup sliced red bell
   pepper
1/2 cup thinly sliced
   carrots
1/2 cup thinly sliced red
   onion
3 tablespoons vegetable
   oil
2 packages chicken
   ramen noodles,
   broken up
1 1/2 cups water

In a small frying pan, toast almonds until lightly browned and then set aside.

In a large frying pan or wok, stir-fry vegetables in oil 3–4 minutes. Add broken noodles and water. Steam 3–5 minutes, or until noodles are done, stirring occasionally. Top with almonds and serve.

Parmesan Noodles

Makes 2–4 servings

**2 packages ramen
   noodles, any flavor**
**1/2 cup grated Parmesan
   cheese**
Salt and pepper, to taste

Cook noodles in water according to package directions and drain. Add Parmesan to warm noodles and stir until cheese is melted. Sprinkle with more Parmesan cheese if desired. Season with salt and pepper.

Beer Noodles

Makes 2 servings

**2 tablespoons vegetable
   oil**
**1 package ramen
   noodles, any flavor,
   broken up**
**1 (10.5-ounce) can onion
   soup, condensed**
1 soup can beer

Heat oil in a medium saucepan over medium heat. Add noodles and lightly brown, stirring constantly. Add soup and beer. Cover and simmer 10 minutes. Drain noodles and serve.

Pepperoni Pizza

Makes 6 servings

8 cups water
4 packages beef ramen noodles, with seasoning packets
1 tablespoon olive oil
6 teaspoons minced garlic
1 teaspoon red pepper flakes
1/2 cup grated fresh Parmesan cheese
1/2 teaspoon oregano
4 eggs
1/2 cup cream
1 cup ricotta cheese
Salt and pepper, to taste
2 cups grated fontina cheese
1 (3.5-ounce) package pepperoni slices

Preheat oven to 425 degrees.

In a large saucepan, bring water to a boil. Add noodles and cook for 3 minutes; drain and set aside. Using a large saucepan, heat olive oil and add the garlic and red pepper flakes, cook and stir for 1 minute. Remove from heat and add the noodles, Parmesan, and oregano. Toss and transfer noodles to a 10¼-inch deep-dish pizza pan that has been prepared with nonstick cooking spray. Spread noodles out evenly to create the crust of the pizza.

Whisk the eggs with the cream and 2 seasoning packets; pour evenly over the noodles. Bake for 5 minutes, or until eggs have set. Meanwhile, season the ricotta with salt and pepper. Remove pan from oven and spread ricotta evenly over the noodles. Sprinkle the fontina cheese on top of the ricotta and top with pepperoni. Return the pan to the oven and increase the temperature to broil. Cook for 5 minutes, or until the cheese has melted and just begins to brown. Cut pizza into wedges and serve.

Cheesy Ranch Ramen

Makes 2–4 *servings*

2 packages finely chopped ramen noodles, any flavor
1 cup ranch dressing
2 cups grated cheddar cheese

Cook noodles in water according to package directions and drain. Add ranch dressing and cheese to noodles and cook over low heat, stirring constantly, until cheese is melted.

Buttery Chive Noodles

Makes 2–4 *servings*

2 packages ramen noodles, any flavor
2 tablespoons butter or margarine
1/2 cup chopped chives
Salt and pepper, to taste

Cook noodles in water according to package directions and drain. Add butter to warm noodles and stir until melted. Add chives and season with salt and pepper.

Desserts

Ramen Trail Mix

Makes 12 cups

**3 packages ramen
noodles, any flavor**

**15 small sticks beef
jerky, cut into small
pieces**

**1/2 pound dried apricots,
cut into small
pieces***

**1/2 cup dried
cranberries,
blueberries,
cherries, or bananas**

**2 cups dry roasted
peanuts**

Break noodles into a bowl. Add
remaining ingredients and stir.

VARIATION: For a more traditional
trail mix, omit the beef jerky and
fruit. Add 1 pound plain M&Ms, 1
cup raisins, 1 cup sunflower seeds,
and 3 cups granola cereal to broken up noodles and stir.

*Any dried fruit combination may
be substituted.

Ramen Haystacks

Makes 4–6 servings

2 cups butterscotch
   chips
1 tablespoon butter
1 tablespoon milk
1 package ramen
   noodles, any flavor,
   crumbled

In a medium saucepan, heat butterscotch, butter, and milk over low heat until chips are completely melted. Stir crumbled, uncooked noodles into butterscotch mixture until coated. Place spoon-sized balls on wax paper, and refrigerate until cool.

Chocolate Chinos

Makes 6–8 servings

2 packages ramen
   noodles, any flavor
3 cups milk chocolate
   chips
2 cups mini
   marshmallows
1/2 cup coconut
1/2 cup chopped walnuts

Preheat oven to 350 degrees.

Do not break noodles. Put blocks of noodles in a lightly greased 8 x 8-inch pan. Cover with layers of chocolate chips and marshmallows. Heat in warm oven until marshmallows and chocolate chips are melted. Layer remaining ingredients over top and refrigerate. When cooled, cut into bars.

Maple and Brown Sugar Ramenmeal

Makes 2 servings

1 package ramen noodles, any flavor
1 cup milk
1 tablespoon syrup
1 tablespoon brown sugar

Crumble ramen into a small microwave-safe bowl. Pour on milk, syrup, and sugar. Heat in the microwave on high 4 minutes, stirring occasionally.

VARIATION: If you'd rather have something fruity, omit the syrup and sugar and add 1 banana, sliced, 1 cup of blueberries, or a mixture of 1/2 cup diced apples, 1 teaspoon cinnamon, and 1 tablespoon sugar.

Chocolate Cherry Cakes

Makes 4 servings

- 1/3 cup vegetable oil
- 1 package ramen noodles, any flavor, finely crushed
- 3 chocolate cupcakes
- 1 cup fresh cherries
- 1/2 cup chocolate fudge, warmed

Heat oil in a large frying pan. Add noodles and fry until lightly brown, stirring constantly; place on paper towels to drain off excess oil.

Break up cake into bite-size pieces. Evenly distribute into 4 serving dishes. Top with cherries and hot fudge. Sprinkle with fried noodles and serve.

Chocolate Ramen Balls

Makes 12 balls

- 4 (1.55-ounce) Nestle Crunch candy bars
- 2 tablespoons milk
- 1 tablespoon honey
- 1 package ramen noodles, any flavor, finely crushed

In a small microwave-safe bowl, combine the candy bars, milk, and honey. Microwave on half power for 1 minute. Stir and repeat until chocolate is melted. Add noodles and mix until thoroughly coated. Spoon tablespoon-size balls onto wax paper. Allow to cool and serve.

Jiggly Ramen

Makes 4–6 servings

1/3 cup vegetable oil
1 package ramen
   noodles, any flavor,
   crushed
2 cups cold water,
   divided
1 (6-ounce) package any
   flavor gelatin

Heat oil in a large frying pan. Add noodles and fry until lightly brown, stirring constantly; place on a paper towels to drain off excess oil.

Bring 1 cup water to a boil in a small saucepan. Add gelatin and stir until completely dissolved. Add remaining water and noodles, stir and transfer to a gelatin mold. Refrigerate for 4 hours or until set. Unmold before serving.

Quick and Easy Fried Ice Cream

Makes 4 servings

1/3 cup vegetable oil
1 package ramen
   noodles, any flavor,
   crushed
1/4 cup brown sugar
1/4 cup chocolate
   sprinkles
4 scoops vanilla ice
   cream

Heat oil in a large frying pan. Add noodles and fry until lightly brown, stirring constantly; place noodles on a paper towel to drain off excess oil.

In a medium bowl, combine noodles with the brown sugar and chocolate sprinkles, toss to mix. Roll each ice cream scoop in mixture and serve.

Choco-Banana Crunch Cakes

Makes 4 servings

4 individual-size sponge cakes

1 large banana, sliced

$1/3$ cup maraschino cherries

1 package ramen noodles, any flavor, crushed

1 cup hot fudge sauce, warmed

Place sponge cakes on individual dessert dishes. Evenly distribute banana slices and cherries between cakes. Sprinkle noodles evenly over cakes and top with hot fudge.

Chocolate Ramen

Makes 1 serving

2 cups water
1 cup brown sugar
1 package ramen
  noodles, any flavor
1 teaspoon vanilla
1 cup chocolate syrup

In a medium saucepan, bring water and brown sugar to a boil. Add noodles and cook for 3 minutes. Reserve 1 tablespoon water and then drain noodles. Add remaining ingredients and reserved water. Toss and serve.

Strawberry Ramen Ice Cream

Makes 4 servings

4 scoops vanilla ice
  cream
1 cup strawberry sauce
1 package ramen
  noodles, any flavor,
  finely crushed

Place ice cream in individual dessert bowls. Top with strawberry sauce and sprinkle with noodles.

Caramel Ramen

Makes 10–15 servings

1/2 cup butter or
  margarine
1/2 cup brown sugar
1/8 teaspoon vanilla
1 tablespoon corn syrup
1 package ramen
  noodles, any flavor,
  finely crushed

Preheat oven to 300 degrees.

Liberally prepare a baking sheet with nonstick cooking spray.

In a small saucepan, mix the butter, brown sugar, vanilla, and corn syrup over medium heat until it starts to bubble and thicken, stirring often; remove from heat. Add noodles and toss to mix. Pour the mixture onto baking sheet and put in the oven for 4 minutes. Remove from the oven and cool in the fridge or freezer. Slice and serve.

White Chocolate Ramen Cookie

Makes 35–40 *balls*

2 tablespoons butter or margarine

3 packages ramen noodles, any flavor, crushed

1 (12-ounce) package white chocolate chips

1/4 cup chopped macadamia nuts

In a large frying pan, melt butter over medium heat. Add noodles and cook until lightly brown.

Melt white chocolate chips in microwave or over a double broiler. Mix the browned noodles and nuts into the melted chocolate. Drop by tablespoonfuls onto wax paper and let set for 20 minutes.

Thin Mint on a Stick

Makes 12

- 1 (8-ounce) bag dark chocolate chips
- 6 drops peppermint extract
- 1 drop spearmint extract
- 1 drop wintergreen extract
- 2 packages ramen noodles, any flavor, crushed
- 12 craft sticks

In a medium saucepan or double boiler, melt the chocolate chips until they become smooth and creamy. Slowly add extracts to the chocolate. Stir for 1 minute. Add noodles and stir vigorously until completely covered. Using a tablespoon, immediately spoon mixture onto wax paper in round cookie shapes. Mixture will flatten and spread considerably, so leave lots of space in between. Place craft stick in each and chill in refrigerator until solid, about 1 hour.

Index